It Don't Mean Nothin' Man

We're Back in the World Now

Jerry W. Whiting

7/13/19
To SHERRY)
REMEMBER OUR VETS.
Jerry Whiting

It Don't Mean Nothin' Man: We're Back in the World Now
Copyright 2017 by Jerry Whiting

First edition

Cover concept by Mark LaScotte
Cover Design by Jim Murphy
Cover painting by Jim Hardy
Original cover painting property of U.S. Army

ISBN 13: 978 – 0971353886

Library of Congress Control Number: 2017903176

Published by
TARNABY
2576 Fox Circle
Walnut Creek, CA 94596
EAJWWhiting@aol.com

PRINTED IN THE UNITED STATES OF AMERICA

Dedication

I dedicate this book to the men and women of the Viet Nam Veterans of Diablo Valley, to the hundreds of thousands of other Americans who chose to serve rather than flee and especially to cousin Ron Dexter and to schoolmate Edgar "Sonny" Flowers and to the more than 58,000 Americans who will remain forever young in our minds. Long live their memories!

Table of Contents

ACKNOWLEDGMENTS

A VERY SPECIAL THANKS TO JOHN REESE, DIRECTOR OF PUBLIC RELATIONS FOR VNVDV FOR PROVIDING THE HISTORY OF HIS ORGANIZATION.

T.D.Barnes
W. Bruce Bartow
John Bybee and SPG
David Behring
Joe Callaway
Tucker Callaway
Bob Caskey
Tom Corbett
Lee Dushkin
Dan Dunn
Charlie Eckwall
Gary Estrella
Dennis Giacovelli
Fred Granados
Bill Green
Peg Green
Jim Hardy
Heather Harris
Jim Hill
Joel Hodge
Bill Holian
Allison Howells
Jeff Jewell
Darrel Kimball
Barbara Kikugawa
Bill Kiper
Rich Lambert
Ray La Rochelle

Bill LaVigne
Carol Long
Norm Mahalich
Kathleen Prevedel Manley
Janette Maring
Mike Martin
Sheree Matousek
Steve Mazaika
Jim Murphy
Casey Nolen
Ron O'Dell
Leif Ortegren
Sherri Ortegren
David Paxton Sr.
Matt Payne
Paul Plumb
Heike Schmidt-Pfeil
Dave Richardson
Jonathan Robbins
Don Schroeder
Mike Slattengren
Dave Smith
Dick Sperling
Bob Tietjen
T.J. Trujillo
Bob Van Noort
Roger Van Noort
Ann Whiting

Foreword One

Let me begin by saying that my family has no military service legacy unless you go back to the Civil War. The Vietnam draft ended when I was in high school and my father and grandfather, respectively, were too young for World War II and World War I. What I do have, however, is a profound respect for all of the men and women who have served this great country over the years. My friend Jerry Whiting has written many wonderful books about our World War II veterans. Now he has completed this book about our local Vietnam veterans – an incredible group of people whose military service stories may be largely unknown, but they have impacted our community with very significant amounts of personal service.

The Vietnam War was starkly different from World War II. It was fought in one country (OK, maybe 3) instead of being a global conflict. The rules of engagement were often dictated by political motives rather than strategic military ones, the reasons for fighting in Vietnam were often opaque instead of the "Good Versus Evil" scenario and in World War II the opposing enemy forces were usually clearly defined instead of a war where guerilla warfare was so pervasive.

One of the most radical differences, however, was in the way we treated our veterans upon their arrival back home. Our World War II veterans were presented with ticker tape parades and hometown celebrations. They were proud to wear their uniforms and speak about their service. Employers welcomed them back and the government passed legislation to assist them with mortgages and college tuition. Our Vietnam veterans, on the other hand, had no celebrations and were often jeered at by members of the public and even World War II veterans for "not winning the war". They had no desire to wear their uniforms in public or tell stories. Many of these men and women were physically, emotionally and psychologically wounded. They had lost so many friends and wondered about the war's justification. Our VA didn't provide enough assistance and many turned to drugs and alcohol to self-medicate. It seemed as though our country wanted to forget about the "defeat" and, in turn, not really acknowledge the men and women who served just as bravely as those that fought in World War II.

In the early 1990's a group of San Ramon Valley veterans decided that they were going to work hard to change the public's perception of them. They established the Viet Nam Veterans of Diablo Valley (VNVDV) and began to meet for fellowship on a monthly basis. As their camaraderie intensified their membership grew. Soon they decided to become heavily involved in the Danville, California Fourth of July Parade. Before long the group became active in both the Veterans Day and Memorial Day ceremonies. In the mid-1990's they came up with the idea of an All Wars Memorial to pay tribute to all of the veterans, as well as the families and friends of the veterans who also endured losses. This unique and beautiful memorial, which was completed in 2005, is a testament to the VNVDV for its driving force and inspiration. They also became an integral part of the renovation and re-design of the Veterans Memorial Building in Danville.

Helping out fellow veterans became another cornerstone of their local service. The VNVDV took on the key role in East Bay Stand Down, a biennial four-day event to assist homeless veterans by providing safe sleeping quarters, new sleeping bags, donated meals, showers and a plethora of other services including drug and alcohol counseling, employment assistance, a "court" where they can have minor offenses removed from their record and medical and dental help. They were also instrumental in the "Welcome Home" project because they wanted every returning service member to be recognized in the future because the Vietnam veterans were not. It is hard not to become emotional when you watch a procession of motorcycles, police vehicles and fire trucks escort a returning veteran to his home where he is met by cheering family members, friends, other veterans and members of the local government. The VNVDV always has a strong presence at these events.

On a more personal note, these men and women are my friends. I especially want to acknowledge Jerry Yahiro, John Reese, Bill Green, Bill Kiper, Ron Lowe and Mike Weber. They care deeply about each other and in helping both the local community and international community. They led several fundraising drives to send wheelchairs back to Vietnam.

In 2012 I had the incredible experience of traveling back to that country with about 20 veterans. The act of providing mobility to a woman who had stepped on a landmine behind her house or placing a man in a wheelchair who suffered from the horrible effects of Agent Orange had a cathartic effect on them. The lively and heartwarming interaction with kids at an orphanage also helped to soothe the nightmarish memories of the war. Meeting former members of the NVA, Vietcong and a two-star general also brought a certain amount of reconciliation to the VNVDV members. In a previous visit to Hanoi, a woman told my veteran friend, "The Americans killed my father during a bombing." As my friend fell silent, she said to him, "It is OK. We were enemies then. We are friends now." One of my most memorable nights was on Ha Long Bay, where I drank and smoked cigars with the guys and heard them exchange stories of their experiences from a half century ago.

Although many of the Vietnam veterans are reluctant to talk about their memories from that time, Jerry has captured a selection of 20+ personal stories filled with courage, humor, friendship and emotion. Bill Kiper, my father-in-law who has a story included in this book, was one of the first Vietnam veterans to really tell me stories about taking off of aircraft carriers at night and worrying about SAMs on his missions over North Viet Nam. I will never forget the tears rolling down his cheeks as he burnished the names of his friends who were on the Viet Nam Memorial.

I hope that Jerry's insight will enhance your respect not only for what they did during a very different war, both on the battlefield and the home front, but also for the way they transformed the shameful way our government and public treated them upon their return into one of the most civic-minded organizations in our country. We commend them for their military service to our country and applaud them for serving our community as citizens in so many valuable ways. Proudly "they" serve.

David Behring
President, Wheelchair Foundation
Board of Directors, All Wars Memorial
Rotarian
Friend of the Viet Nam Veterans of Diablo Valley

FIG 1 - DAVID BEHRING, STANDING CENTER WITH VIET NAM VETERANS OF DIABLO VALLEY DELIVERING WHEELCHAIRS IN VIETNAM.

Foreword Two

As a former veteran's benefits counselor for a large county in California and director/counselor for Veterans Affairs with the Vet Centers for over 30 years, I have worked with hundreds of Vietnam veterans and their families dealing with the wounds of war. Jerry Whiting's book captures what it was like for Veterans returning from the Vietnam War-how they were treated, how they adjusted and how they stuck together.

It Don't Mean Nothin' Man: We're Back in the World Now tells the story of 20+ members of the Viet Nam Veterans of Diablo Valley, their struggles in dealing with the aftermath of war, and how it changed their lives. In each story Jerry shows the impact the Vietnam War had on individual lives, their loved ones, families and co-workers. The book paints a vivid picture of what the veterans have accomplished both in their community and in their individual lives. It is well established that the Vietnam veterans have contributed to Society by raising families, volunteering in the community, working in honorable professions, becoming political leaders, as well as becoming protectors of their fellow wounded veterans and the infirmed.

Vietnam veterans were the first ones to stand up in this community and publicly talk about their mistreatment. As a result of their efforts a trail has been blazed for generations of veterans to receive better treatment, respect and honor from not only the Department of Veterans Affairs, but the nation as a whole. In my experience, and what is so eloquently stated in Jerry's book, is that Vietnam veterans have always taken responsibility to be good citizens. I am reminded of a quote from Viktor Frankl, who was a holocaust survivor. In his book *Man's Search for Meaning*, which I truly believe personifies Vietnam veterans, he said, "Ultimately, man should not ask what the meaning of his life is, but rather must recognize that it is he who is asked. In a word, each man is questioned by life; and he can only answer to life by answering for his own life; to life he can only respond by being responsible."

Having spent the last years helping veterans and their family members, it is a pleasure to recommend you read such an uplifting book. Get ready to be amazed by Jerry Whiting's writing ability to tell the stories of these incredible Vietnam War veterans.

Jeffrey L. Jewell
Vet Center Director
U. S. Dept. of Veterans Affairs
Concord Vet Center
Concord, CA

FIG 2 - JEFF JEWELL 1980

FIG 3 - JEFF JEWELL TODAY

Foreword Three

"Ending a conflict is not so simple, not just calling it off and coming home. Because the price for that kind of peace could be a thousand years of darkness for generation's Vietnam borned." (Ronald Reagan)

To the Viet Nam Veterans of Diablo Valley,

It has been an emotional journey for me as a war orphan of this unpopular conflict. The effects and devastation of the war, the loss of my biological family, and its aftermath profoundly hindered me, constantly lingering in the distance, memories of a frightened, fragile child.

My reflections and memory of American troops, and their compassion toward us forgotten orphans, through their gentle touch and gift of time are fondly held within my heart with the highest regard and respect. It is with much gratitude and appreciation that I thank you for my beloved adopted country and my freedom; for the vital principals that you taught me through your example of courage and strength by your unwavering service to your country.

Cảm ơn (Vietnamese for "thank you for") touching my soul, for your inspiration, for your unconditional love and compassion for the children and people of the Republic of Viet Nam. Thank you for permitting me to shed the tears buried within my soul; to express my sorrow and grieve with you for your loss; and to finally, convey to you that I am forever indebted to you and for all that you have sacrificed. I offer you a special tribute and gratitude for your efforts in preserving history by sharing these personal experiences, sacrifices, and stories.

With much love and gratitude,

Janette Maring

Former Orphan of Tu Tam Orphanage, Pleiku, RVN

FIG 4 - JANETTE AT TU TAM ORPHANAGE (1970) WITH MEN FROM THE 52ND AVIATION BRIGADE

FIG 5 - JANETTE AND HER FAMILY

(Author's note: Janette's parents and family were killed in Vietnam and she was placed in Tu Tam orphanage. She was adopted by a Vietnamese family and was eventually able to flee Vietnam by boat and make her way to the U.S. Janette is married and she and her husband and four children live in Michigan.)

Foreword Four

Less than a week after I was crowned Miss World in 1969 I was on my way to L.A. to prepare for the Bob Hope Christmas tour. I'm still not certain why I was invited to join the tour, but it was a memorable and exciting experience for a 20-year-old woman from the small town of Bruck, Austria.

Our home base for our tour in Southeast Asia was Bangkok, Thailand, and from here we ventured out to several bases in Vietnam by Chinook helicopter, always returning to Bangkok at the end of the day. As a child I was a tomboy so I found it quite an adventure to be flying through the Vietnamese countryside in an American military helicopter that had door gunners with machineguns. Our helicopter was never hit but we did see smoke from firing in the distance.

We went to 5 or 6 bases in Vietnam to entertain you Americans who were so far away from home. We also gave a performance on the aircraft carrier USS Ranger. I had heard of Bob Hope before the tour because of his "Road" films, but I didn't know about his tour before I was invited to participate. I had never heard of actress/singer Connie Stevens or of the Gold Diggers song and dance troupe. I became acquainted with them on the tour. There was one person on the tour whose name was familiar to me, astronaut Neil Armstrong, who had landed on the moon a few months earlier. This made for an interesting group of people as travel companions. Since my English was very limited in those days, I didn't talk so much to the other entertainers.

I have many memories of this trip, but some of the most powerful are of our visits to hospitals. At each stop along the way we visited wounded soldiers at the base hospitals. We saw the effects of war on these brave young men, some of whom had missing limbs. They were always happy to see us. We were told ahead of time to not let our emotions show in front of them, but sometimes I cried after we left the hospitals. The less seriously wounded also attended our performances, usually seated near the front of the stage in wheelchairs, wearing pajamas.

I will never forget that tour and the thousands of American troops who attended our shows. I met just a few, but heard the cheers of the others. For those who saw me in 1969, it was a privilege to entertain you. I applaud all of you for your service and I am happy that your stories are being preserved in this book.

All the best to you and your families,

Eva Rueber-Staier Cowan

Miss World 1969

Fig 6 - Eva with Bob Hope 1969 and Eva today

Introduction

It was in the fall of 1970 that I first met Ed. I was a student at the University of California, Santa Barbara and was living in an apartment on the beach. I had just transferred there and didn't know many people.

The first time I saw him was early in the morning, about 6 AM. I couldn't sleep and got up early to watch the sunrise and ocean from the balcony. Ed was definitely a surfer, very tan, of medium stature. He had long, thick hair bleached blond by the sun and a thick, reddish-colored beard. He was standing at the edge of the cliff beneath the balcony, holding his surfboard, watching the waves, wearing cut off faded camouflage military fatigue pants and tan-colored flip flops. I soon learned that he was my neighbor.

I didn't realize it then, but a couple of things about Ed seemed different and stood out from your average surfer of the day. He stood straighter than most surfers I saw and, when he later talked to me, he always made eye contact and looked directly at me. I spoke to him several times in passing before we actually had a conversation. Like many other surfers in those days, Ed drove an old, dilapidated VW bus and one of our first conversations was about his bus. I noted it hadn't been moved for several days and asked if something was wrong with it. He told me the engine blew up. He said he didn't have any money to fix it and mentioned in the same conversation that he had missed his enrollment at Santa Barbara City College. I made a comment about his recent misfortunes and said something like "That's terrible". He looked off into the distance, toward the ocean and answered, "Don't mean nothin' man…..don't mean nothin'." It was then that I understood a little more about him. He was a Vietnam Vet. I had heard the phrase before, but only from returning Vets.

As I got to know Ed a little better during the next few weeks, he eventually told me he recently returned from Vietnam, where he had served three years in the Marine Corps. He was released a few weeks early to enroll in school, but had somehow missed the enrollment and had to wait until the next semester. There was a problem with finances until he could start school, but he seemed happy just to be surfing. Ed never mentioned the Marine Corps or Vietnam again. He was up before dawn every day, standing at the edge of the cliff with his surfboard before he made his way down to the beach and paddled out to sea. I didn't have the impression that he was running from his past experiences. He didn't strike me as the kind of guy who would run from anything. It seemed to me that he was just adjusting.

Ed eventually obtained a used engine from a junkyard and knowing that I occasionally worked on cars, he asked if I could help him put the engine in his car. I agreed to swap engines in the VW, in exchange for a case of cheap, generic beer. He was thrilled to have the bus running again so he could venture farther along the coast and find better surfing spots. I was happy to have the beer as it gave me some status with my new roommates, so it was a good deal for us both. A few months later Ed and his VW were gone. I have no idea where he went, but he moved on. I never knew Ed's last name. I hope he found peace and happiness.

A few years ago I learned about this group called the Viet Nam Veterans of Diablo Valley. I heard about the many good things they were doing in the community, without any fanfare and without any politics. I met a few of them on different occasions and at different events. I had written a book about some local WWII Vets and wondered why someone hadn't written a similar book about this group. My friends David Behring and Dan Dunn apparently had similar thoughts and brought this up one day, suggesting I write a book about some of the Vets in this group and about the group itself. I thought more about it, even consulting a couple of the Vets in the group. After talking to David again, I agreed to write the book.[1]

This project has been different from other book projects. For my WWII book projects I was an outsider because I wasn't even born until several years after the war ended. This would be a book that was more about my generation. During this war I was of military age, but didn't serve. How would the Vets react to an outsider who "could" have been there, but wasn't? Would they trust me enough to share their stories with me? Would they trust me to write about them?

The first time I met them as a group was when I was invited to speak to them about one of my WWII book projects. About 80 of them had gathered for their monthly dinner meeting. I was confident in speaking to them about that topic, but was apprehensive about how they would accept me at a different level. Bill Green and Mike Martin were the first Vets to welcome me and my book concept/project. They spearhead the Speakers Bureau for the group and are some of the most visible faces of the group. They invited me to attend one of their presentations. Naturally, I accepted and they made me feel welcome. After that Bill invited me repeatedly to afternoon scotch and cigar sessions in his backyard, where some of the Vets gathered to relax. The more comfortable I felt, the more I began to feel that this project could succeed. When Bill shared his Vietnam journal with me I knew I had his trust and my confidence grew even more.

I wasn't quite sure of the meaning of "It don't mean nothin'", but thought it might be a good title for my book. At times and in the course of conversations with other Vietnam Vets in the late 60's, I took it to mean that, whatever the issue was, it wasn't a big deal or something like "Don't sweat the small stuff". On other occasions, when I heard it used in a different context, I thought it meant that nothing was a big deal or nothing was important in life. I thought that perhaps compared to those war experiences, nothing could seem as important. I could not have been more wrong. It may mean different things to different Vets, but all have told me it was a positive phrase, more of a celebration of life and survival, more like my original thought, "Don't sweat the small stuff. You're alive!"

Another phrase I heard only from returning Vietnam Vets was their reference to being "back in the world". I came to know that this was what they longed for, returning home to the USA. As I searched for meaningful titles and subtitles for this book, I asked some of the Vets for suggestions. I spoke to Jerry Yahiro, one of the Vets, one day at a scotch and cigar session and he reminded me that most of the Vets longed to be "back in the world", and this was a term every Vietnam

Vet would know, so it became my subtitle. Maybe the meanings of the phrases aren't as important as the fact that these are their phrases, just as this is their book.

Many of their stories are not about combat, but all of them served their country. Not all volunteered, but all served. None of them ran to Canada to escape service. All are proud of their service, and should be. You will not read about medals and decorations in this book. I intentionally left this out. Many of the men in the stories were highly decorated, some for actions described in this book, but they were often the first to point out that courageous acts are often not observed or recognized. One said it simply, "We all served", and suggested strongly that I remember this. I have. There may be endnote references to citations as my source of information; otherwise you won't read about medals.[2]

Many who served in Vietnam were not in combat, despite the fact that no place was safe there. Some of those who were regularly in the most intense combat situations chose to speak of other things, not wanting to relive those experiences. For example, T.J. Trujillo saw a lot of combat as an infantryman, yet he asked me if I was going to include any humorous stories in the book. I told him I would like to include a humorous story if I found an appropriate one. He shared one and that is the one you will read about. Bill Green was also an infantryman who spent nearly his entire year in the "boonies", in combat. The story I chose to include about him is a love story.

The reader should keep in mind that these are short stories, chosen to represent unique and individual personal experiences in the Vietnam War, often lasting just a few minutes. They are brief glimpses into the lives of these Vets, while most were there a year or more. An entire book could be written about each of them.

You'll also read about the unsettling times and the condition of our country when these men returned home. It's all part of our history. Of equal importance, you'll read of some of the things this group continues to do, individually and collectively, to make our communities and our world a better place.

One recurring theme that surfaced during several of my interviews is the concern these Vets have for the memories of those who didn't return home. It surfaced in various ways. Sometimes it began with a hesitation in the telling of a story of a combat situation where a buddy was killed. In other cases it was simply a conversation about a serviceman who was killed or one who is still missing, often accompanied by a comment that we need to remember those who were lost. During several other interviews the Vets spoke about meeting with children or relatives of a buddy who was killed, sometimes recently, to give them answers and to provide information about the lost loved one. You won't hear the Vets talking openly about this, but it surfaced repeatedly during several interviews. We must honor their memories.

I've come to realize that it wasn't easy for some of these Veterans to share their experiences. As I mentioned, in some cases Vets who saw extensive combat chose to share stories that weren't directly related to combat. I made no attempt to pry or enter places where I was not welcome. The responses I got from the Vets when I shared drafts of their stories with them were revealing. One commented that it was "startling and slightly unsettling" to see his story in print, yet he liked it.

I quickly learned that this generation, my generation, is less trusting than the WWII generation. Having written several books about men who served in WWII, in the early stages of this project it became obvious to me that the WWII generation was more open. When I had written chapter drafts about WWII Vets I interviewed and offered the draft to a Vet for a review, those Vets generally were satisfied to see their stories for the first time when the book was in print. From the onset it was obvious that the Vietnam Vets, as a group, weren't as trusting. Several made it clear that they wanted to see what I had written before it appeared in a book. With this in mind, in each case I asked the Vet to review the draft. This served a dual purpose. It assured accuracy in the story. Often the Vet would think of additional details that weren't covered in the original interview. Perhaps more importantly, it helped to build a more trusting relationship. This was very beneficial to me, because I'm sure the word got around to some of the others that I could be trusted. This "trust phenomenon" isn't unique to just Vets from my generation. Most of us are less trusting of the news media, in general, and of information that is made public about us.[3]

As the project progressed and my interviews continued, Vets approached me and volunteered to share their stories and experiences. Their trust and confidence in me was building and at this point I knew the project wouldn't fail. In the end, there were many others who would have shared experiences with me, but then this project would have been volumes, instead of a single book.

Each Veteran and each interview stands out to me for a different reason. One Vet, who was particularly candid when describing a combat experience, told me he didn't tell his wife he was a Vietnam Vet until a few years after he was married. She knew he had served in the military, but he hadn't told her he'd been in Vietnam. Another Vet shared an intensely personal story with me near the end of a long interview. After he finished the story he looked at me and said he had never told this story before. I asked him if I could choose this story for inclusion in the book and he agreed, then told me that he also wanted to share the story with his wife before the book came out so it wouldn't be a surprise to her.

This is not just a book of memoirs. Wherever possible, I attempted to obtain official documents or other verification of the information told to me. I did this not because I didn't trust the story, but because I felt an obligation to protect the Veteran if the information was questioned in any way. This wasn't always possible, but most of the time the information could be confirmed. I found no evidence that any of the stories were embellished that were told to me; more often than not it was just the opposite and they were downplayed. If there are errors in any factual information presented I assume full responsibility.

I hope you honor these Vets for what they have done and what they stand for. I'm extremely proud of them and it is my pleasure to present their stories. I'm particularly honored they trusted me and grateful for the friendships that developed. My hope is that my prodding into those difficult times in the past hasn't caused them undue hardships. I've made some new friends and will always be grateful for this. There are some accounts of extreme bravery in the book, but all are stories of extreme service to their community and to their country.

Vietnam was a difficult time period in our nation's history, with increasing criticism and unpopularity as the war continued. I would ask that you think of the word courage as you read the stories. Courage takes many forms and I saw various aspects of courage as I interviewed the Vets, ranging from the raw courage in battle situations to the courage it took to move forward in life, sometimes standing alone, without the support and respect of a seemingly ungrateful nation. Perhaps there is courage in returning to Vietnam years later, facing those memories of war, while delivering wheelchairs to children impacted by that war and meeting a former enemy. Or maybe there is courage in just getting up every day, with the physical pain of injuries from a war long ago, or in facing repeated bouts of cancer caused by Agent Orange, the defoliant to which many Vets were exposed. I hope you enjoy the book.

NOTES AND REFERENCES

[1] The earlier book written about WWII is titled, ***Veterans in the Mist: Memoirs of the Third Thursday Lunch Bunch.***

[2] Some of the bravest actions documented in this book received no recognition at all.

[3] I made a commitment at the onset that I would not include any story in the book if the Vet didn't approve of it. If we couldn't come to an agreement, I would simply give the story to the Vet if he or she wanted it and it wouldn't be included in the book. This never happened.

Prologue

As he slowly and carefully walked down the path, he couldn't help but reflect on his first tour in Vietnam. Jerry Yahiro was a new 2nd lieutenant then. So much had changed. The Special Forces camp here at Ben Het was different, too.

FIG 7 - LT. JERRY YAHIRO

Jerry was born on Maui and grew up there. After high school he enrolled at Seattle University on the mainland and got a degree in Political Science. While there he enrolled in Army R.O.T.C. and received his commission upon graduation in 1966. After further training he was landed in Vietnam in June of 1967. By this time things were really heating up in Vietnam.

Jerry was assigned to the 3rd Battalion, 12th Infantry Regiment, 4th Infantry Division as a mortar platoon leader in the Central Highlands. He spent much of his time at his battalion fire base, providing fire support with his mortars for the infantrymen in the field. During the first week of November the Special Forces camp at Ben Het requested assistance and he and about a dozen of his men with three 81 MM mortars were sent to give them a hand.

This base was just a few miles from both the Laotian and Cambodian borders, in an area they called the tri-border area, just inside the boundaries of Vietnam. The Special Forces camp operated independently most of the time, but occasionally called for help from other units. The Ho Chi Minh Trail, which delivered supplies and manpower from North Vietnam, was just across the border, and technically off-limits to the Americans. The main purpose of the camp was to

Fig 8 - Combat ready Lt. Yahiro

interdict the North Vietnamese as they tried to enter South Vietnam. There had recently been more enemy activity in this area, a clear sign that something bigger was brewing. The Special Forces guys, the Green Berets, wanted help from his mortars to protect the base and to provide fire support when they contacted enemy forces within 3 or 4 miles of the base, where Jerry's mortars were a very effective tool.

Jerry and his men stayed at Ben Het for six days. They kept busy during that time period. Throughout the day and night the mortars were used for harassment and interdiction, firing on likely routes the North Vietnamese may be using to enter the area. There were also daily fire missions, in direct support of the Green Berets and their Montagnard support forces who came into direct contact with the North Vietnamese forces. The base also took some fire at night, but nothing major and nothing very close to Jerry and his men.[1]

On November 12th, Jerry and his team returned to their battalion fire base where there was plenty of enemy activity. For more than 20 days a major battle raged in this region, a battle that became known as the Battle of Dak To.

Now he was back again in Vietnam, with mixed feelings. He wasn't with his own men from the 4th Infantry this time. It was the same time of year, November. The 90-degree heat and 70% humidity was the same, hot and humid, very sticky. The North Vietnamese hadn't been able to overrun Ben Het in '67, a good thing. The Green Berets held strong, assisted by his mortars. Jerry walked down the dirt road, his thoughts drifting to the earlier tour, his two companions behind him, letting him take the lead. He tried to focus on the present situation.

Suddenly the sounds of automatic weapons fire erupted in the distance in front of him, followed by other loud explosions, likely mortar fire. For just a moment he stopped in his tracks, his face turning ashen gray. Not again! He regained his composure quickly, realizing it couldn't be. This was 2012, not 1967.[2]

The companions behind Jerry were his wife, Patti, and a tour guide. His mission to Vietnam this time was delivering wheelchairs to needy people in Vietnam, part of The Wheelchair Foundation and one of the many worthy causes supported by members of the Viet Nam Veterans of Diablo Valley. Jerry and Patti had been in the Saigon area with their group, but Jerry wanted to return to the area where he had served so many years ago.

They took a short flight to Pleiku, where they had met their guide and drove through the region to Ben Het. The fire they heard was from a nearby military training base, but for that brief moment, he was 2nd Lt. Jerry Yahiro again.[3]

FIG 9 - JERRY YAHIRO TODAY

NOTES AND REFERENCES

[1] The Montagnards lived in the Central Highlands of Vietnam. They were recruited and trained by U.S. Special Forces in the region and fought alongside the Americans.

[2] The details for this story came from an interview with Jerry Yahiro on 10/16/15.

[3] The Wheelchair Foundation, a non-profit, has as its mission to provide wheelchairs to every child, teen and adult in the world who needs one but can't afford one. To date, they have provided more than one million wheelchairs, most in developing nations. The Viet Nam Veterans of Diablo Valley actively supports the program. Jerry had also returned to Vietnam in 2006, delivering wheelchairs.

Chapter One

Courage in Elephant Valley

Norm Mahalich walked into his real estate office in Danville, California and saw a paperback book on his desk that someone had obviously left for him. It was a book about recon Marines in Vietnam, entitled *Never Without Heroes: Marine Third Reconnaissance Battalion in Vietnam, 1965-1970.* Whomever left the book there must have known that Norm's cousin was in this unit, was killed and is still listed as MIA. Norm was a Vietnam Vet himself, a Marine helicopter pilot in VMO-2 (Marine Observation Squadron 2) on his first tour and later a C-130 pilot on his second tour. He took the book home with him, but didn't feel like reading a book that would likely evoke some of those past memories. Even though it was 1997, and 32 years since he had been there in 1965 on his first tour, he didn't feel ready to open the doors on some of those memories.[1]

Several months later Norm picked up the book and looked through the index. Sure enough, on page 364, there was a reference to his cousin, Dennis Christie. As he leafed through the book his thoughts took him back to 1966, to a place called Elephant Valley, and to his own interactions with some very brave recon Marines and, particularly to their platoon leader. What was his name, again? Norm never met this man, but he did speak to him on the radio, saw him running on the ground, and couldn't forget his bravery. He was in this recon battalion in the book and, after some thought recalled that his last name was something like Laterra. As he looked at the book his thoughts took him back to that day, February 22, 1966.[2]

Before Vietnam Norm attended Glendale Junior College in California for a couple of years and enlisted in the Marine Corps as a cadet, with the intention of becoming a pilot. After

FIG 10-MARINE CADET MAHALICH

training in both fixed wing aircraft and helicopters he found himself a 23 year-old 1st lieutenant in Vietnam, flying primarily UH-1E Huey gunships. This version of the helicopter had four fixed forward firing M60 machineguns, two forward firing rocket pods (each carrying 18 rockets) and two door-mounted M60 machineguns. The pilot operated the forward firing machineguns and rockets, while the door gunner operated one of the other M60's and the crew chief operated the other. He arrived in the spring of 1965 and was an experienced combat pilot within a few short weeks. His unit was based at the Marble Mountain Air Facility, just a few miles southeast of Da Nang.[3]

On this particular day he and his copilot, Doug Page, had just returned from a combat mission in the late afternoon. As they walked to the mess hall an enlisted man ran up to them, excited, and told them there was an emergency, that a Marine patrol engaged a large enemy force, was pinned down and they needed to report to the operations room to get more information to support the Marines. Page and Norm ran to the operations area where they met the designated flight leader, Captain Robert Smith. Smith said the situation was urgent and they needed to take off immediately. He'd brief them on the radio while enroute to the location in Elephant Valley, which was northwest of Da Nang.

Norm and Page ran to their helicopter with the crew chief and door gunner. They took off, armed with 3600 rounds of ammunition and 36 rockets. After take-off, they checked in with DASC (Direct Air Support Command), a control center on the ground, to let them know that two gunships were on their way to assist the Marine patrol. Captain Smith provided the needed information over the radio. Their squadron commander, Lt. Col. George Bauman, was on scene with one other gunship, piloted by Captain James Rider. Both gunships had been supplying fire support to the beleaguered Marines on the ground, but Bauman was running out of fuel and needed immediate relief. The weather turned bad with a heavy overcast and fixed wing aircraft couldn't get near enough to provide the needed close-in support.

The situation on the ground was critical. Although they didn't have all of the details, this is what occurred. A 17-man Marine reconnaissance patrol, led by 1st Lt. Joe Laterra, had moved into a position late in the afternoon where they prepared to spend the night. They set up a perimeter defense and began to receive automatic weapons fire from all directions. Laterra got the patrol up and moving, headed to an open area where they intended to be extracted the following day by helicopters. They were under fire as they moved through the thick, triple canopy jungle. At times the enemy, North Vietnamese regulars, were as close as 30' from the patrol. The NVA even yelled at them in broken English, in the midst of shooting and lobbing grenades, with comments like "Yankee go home" and "Long live Vietnam".

Large numbers of enemy were seen in different directions, including one group of more than 30, and the fire was intense. It was suspected they may have come across a battalion-sized force of several hundred North Vietnamese regular army troops.[4]

FIG 11- LT. JOE LATERRA (IN FRONT) WITH RECON TEAM

Laterra's radioman was able to establish contact with the 3rd Recon base camp and requested assistance and extraction before dark, since they were outgunned and seriously outnumbered. Bauman and Rider arrived with their gunships to provide close air support. Both were able to keep the patrol from being overrun, shooting their rockets and machineguns for more than an hour. Now they were both out of ammo, Bauman was nearly out of fuel, and fog was settling in. It was now nearly 6:00 PM and it would be dark before too long. This was the situation as Norm and Smith approached.[5]

Smith called Norm on the radio and said his FM radio wasn't working. This was the radio that provided communications to the Marines on the ground. He asked Norm if he could make contact with the Marines on the ground and Norm did so, verifying he had established contact. At that point Smith asked Norm to take over the flight lead position. As the two gunships approached the valley Norm saw the other two gunships circling the area of the engagement. He directed Smith to continue circling out of the immediate area and flew into the valley himself to determine exactly where the Marines were and to get a situation report from Lt. Col Bauman. After getting the update the other two Hueys quickly left the scene, turning over control to Norm.

About this time Norm heard three UH-34 troop transport helicopters on the UHF radio, checking in with the control center. He immediately declared an emergency, explaining the situation and diverting these three helicopters to his location. On the FM radio he told the Marines on the ground, call sign "Recon Alpha 3", that help was on the way and he and Captain Smith began strafing the area around where the Marines were pinned down. He wouldn't use his rockets because the enemy was too close to the Marines and he was afraid he'd hit them, but his machineguns kept the enemy at bay.

FIG 12 -NORM MAHALICH IN HIS HUEY

Within a few minutes the UH-34s approached, call sign "Tarbush". There wasn't much room in the narrow valley so Norm relayed the plan to the Tarbush flight that the troop helicopters would go in one at a time, escorted by Norm and Smith on either side, the gunships suppressing the ground fire while the UH-34 picked up Marines. The plan was relayed to the Marines on the ground and they were told to have five men ready to go.

The gunships made at least two passes, strafing the areas close to the Marines on the ground and these Marines were also laying down fire, while Tarbush 1 descended, approaching the landing zone. As Tarbush 1 approached, one of the NVA ran into the clearing directly in front of the helicopter and began firing at pointblank range at the helicopter. He was immediately shot by one of the Marines on the ground. Five Marines jumped into the helicopter and it slowly lurched forward, overloaded. Norm watched as it struggled to take off and lumbered down the valley, now accompanied by the two gunships on either side, firing as they went.

Fire was coming from 360 degrees and the Marines on the ground were completely surrounded. As the UH-34 left the area, the pilot radioed he had nearly crashed and was overloaded and that the other helicopters should only pick up four Marines. Norm passed this info down to the Marines on the ground and received an acknowledgment.[6]

Tarbush 2 and 3 repeated the efforts of Tarbush 1, with the gunships supplying deadly accurate fire, making pass after pass over the enemy positions. Eight more Marines were evacuated. Now the troop-carrying helicopters had left the area, with four Marines still on the ground. The enemy fire on the ground became more intense, with the North Vietnamese moving closer. Lt. Laterra told his Marines to fix bayonets, knowing it would soon be hand-to-hand combat with this overwhelming force of enemy troops. The situation seemed hopeless, but the Marines weren't quitting. At this point the radio operator keyed the radio, under the direction of the platoon leader and told Norm to strafe his position. Norm answered that he wouldn't do that, not yet. The radio operator answered that he'd "get a lot of them" if he did and that it couldn't get much worse than the fire they were already receiving.

At this point Norm realized the only chance the Marines had was to get them out himself in his gunship. With Smith covering him, this was still a longshot. All knew there was little chance of survival if they went in. He told the Marines he was coming in to get them. He knew there was no possibility they could hold out until the next day and would soon be overrun.

Norm pulled off to the side and dropped his rocket pods to make the ship lighter. He told the crew to throw everything out except ammo. He glanced quickly back and, as he did so, both Marine door gunners gave him a "thumbs up" signal. He looked to his left at Doug Page in the copilot's seat and Doug nodded at him. Damn, these guys were brave! He wasn't certain he could lift off with the weight of four additional men in the Huey, but he could at least make the effort. He radioed to Smith his intention, requesting cover fire and both helicopters descended into the valley, guns firing.

As Norm approached the landing zone he heard another voice on the radio. It was Tarbush 1 calling in, saying he'd dropped the five Marines out of the area in a safe place and was coming back for the others. Fantastic! Once again Norm relayed this information to the Marines and told them to get in their holes and keep their heads down. He hovered about 50' off the ground, about 100 yards off to the side of the Marines' position, laying down cover fire directly on top of the Marines' positions. Both door gunners were blazing away at the NVA on the ground who were near the Marines. In the hover Norm turned the helicopter from side to side, raking the entire area with machinegun fire, until the guns were empty, while Captain Smith did the same announcing "ammo minus" to tell his crew when the ammo was exhausted. He watched happily and in amazement when the four Marines jumped up and ran from their cover positions, with bayonets fixed and jumped into the UH-34. The two gunships escorted the UH-34 out of the danger zone, enemy guns firing at them as they left and flew back to their base at Marble Mountain. It was just another day in the life of a Marine Huey gunship pilot. It was already dark when they landed.

The next day, when Norm returned to base after another mission, one of the guys told him he'd had a visitor. Norm asked who it was and the Marine said "It was some grunt lieutenant by the name of Laterra".

It was only then that he learned the name of that platoon leader, that brave Marine who had called the fire in on himself. The Marine said, "He wanted to thank you for his continuing life."

FIG 13-LT. JOE LATERRA

Not one of those 17 Marines received a scratch that day. It was one of those miracles that came out of war. He was proud of those Marines on the ground and proud of his crew and the crews of those other six helicopters who braved the withering fire to rescue some fellow Marines.[7]

As Norm looked through the book he'd received, reminded of that incident long ago, he decided to try to find Laterra. First he contacted author Lawrence Vetter, to see if he might know Joseph Laterra. Vetter said he thought Laterra lived somewhere on the East Coast. Norm did a little searching and eventually located Laterra in Rhode Island. Norm phoned and left a message with Laterra's wife. Laterra phoned back, not knowing that Norm was one of the pilots who rescued him and his men that day. When Laterra asked why Norm called, he answered that he was one of the men who gave him his "continuing life". A long conversation followed, followed by letters back and forth. The two men talked of getting together, and Norm finally met Joe Laterra in Arizona in January 2016, where Joe was vacationing. They spent two days together, reminiscing and enjoying each other's company.

Norm left the Marine Corps in 1968 and began a career as a commercial airline pilot, flying for TWA. He was also a real estate broker in Contra Costa County. He and his wife, Lily, raised one son. Today Norm is retired and he and Lily live in Placerville, California. Norm is the founder of Viet Nam Veterans of Diablo Valley. He was a driving force behind the creation of the All Wars Memorial in Danville, California and is a lifetime member in the VFW.[8]

FIG 14-NORM MAHALICH TODAY

NOTES AND REFERENCES

[1]*Lawrence C. Vetter Jr, Never Without Heroes: Marine Third Reconnaissance Battalion in Vietnam, 1965*-70 (New York, NY: Ballantine Books, 1996)

[2] The date was confirmed by an entry in Mahalich's flight log as well as by the Patrol Report from 3rd Platoon, Company A, 3rd Reconnaissance Battalion for that date and the 1965-1966 VMO-2 Chronology.

[3] Mahalich also flew Medevac Hueys on a regular basis and occasionally flew the O-1 Bird Dog aircraft, a Cessna used for observation.

[4] The source of this information about the recon mission is from the Patrol Report, 3rd Platoon, Company A, 3rd Reconnaissance Battalion for 2/22/66, as well as a written statement by Joseph Laterra, dated 4/3/02. The quotes are

directly from the recon mission report. The suspected size of the force was referenced both in the 3rd Recon Patrol Report and the 1965-1966 VMO-2 Chronology.

[5] James W. Rider provided information about what occurred before Mahalich arrived in a written statement, dated 8/22/02.

[6] The specific information about the enemy soldier in the LZ was in the Patrol Report, completed by Lt. Laterra at the end of the mission.

[7] Details of the mission and specifically of Laterra's visit to thank the Marine pilots are from a letter that copilot Doug Page wrote to his wife, dated 2/23/66.

[8] Mahalich was interviewed on 11/11/15 and 11/2/15 by the author. Three phone interviews followed. These interviews are the source of his personal account, as well as a written statement he made on 10/1/01, describing in detail what happened on the mission. In addition, Joe Laterra was interviewed in 12/15, confirming details provided by Norm Mahalich.

Chapter Two

First In at Night

Their numbers were small in Vietnam. They were a highly specialized group of men known as Pathfinders. Their history dates back to WWII, when our military saw the need to insert specially trained troops into enemy territory before an invasion. They could be inserted by various means, including boat, but they often entered from the air. In fact, the first Americans on land during the Normandy invasion were Pathfinders who parachuted into France before other airborne troops several hours before the invasion itself.

In South Vietnam, American troops already had a strong presence by the mid-1960s. There were no invasions, but there were plenty of air assaults into enemy-held territory. These air assaults were accomplished primarily with helicopter-carrying troops. This is where the Pathfinders played an important role.[1]

Their role was to find the most practical and safest landing zones for the troop-carrying Huey helicopters. This would also include the safest approach lanes to the landing zones (LZ's) and departure routes. Sometimes they would be dropped in as much as a day ahead of time to prepare for the air assault, but most of the time they were inserted the same day.

Jim Hill was not a Pathfinder when he arrived in Vietnam in January 1966. His main base was at Cu Chi and he was initially a rifle platoon leader in B Company, 1st battalion, 27th Infantry Regiment, 25th Infantry Division. Then he became a weapons platoon leader in a mortar platoon and finally the executive officer for the rifle company. He saw plenty of combat in these assignments during his first six months in Vietnam.[2]

Fig 15 - Lt. Jim Hill in Vietnam

Jim was born in Washington D.C. and raised in Virginia. He graduated from Fairfax High School in Fairfax, Virginia. He attended and graduated from the University of Richmond, Virginia in 1964 with a B.S. degree in Business Administration. While there he enrolled in R.O.T.C. and was a Distinguished Military Graduate. He was offered, and accepted, a Regular Army commission with a 4-year commitment. He attended Airborne and Ranger training and was then assigned to the 25th Infantry Division, before going to Vietnam.

An interesting sidelight to Jim's story is a series of whirlwind events that occurred after he graduated. He graduated from college, received his commission, attended a graduation function in Richmond, Virginia, drove 90 miles to get married in Culpepper, Virginia and then drove 560 miles to report to his first duty assignment at Ft. Knox Kentucky, all within 48 hours.

FIG 16 - JIM HILL ON ARMORED PERSONNEL CARRIER

About six months into his year-long tour in Vietnam he was back at division headquarters when he saw a posting on the bulletin board requesting volunteers for a Pathfinder group that was being formed in-country for the 25th Infantry Division. Early combat operations in Vietnam demonstrated the need for Pathfinders, for men to go in ahead of the helicopters and to reconnoiter the landing zone and prepare the LZ for the incoming helicopter-borne troops and direct them in and out.

Some of the other units already had Pathfinder detachments and were beginning to use them extensively. The 25th Infantry Division had no such unit. In spite of its fairly recent arrival it was the largest infantry division in Vietnam at the time. Jim thought he was a good fit for this assignment and immediately volunteered. Unlike most of the division officers, he had already successfully graduated from Airborne and Ranger training schools. An eligibility requirement for Pathfinder training was being "jump qualified". Having become a Ranger was a bonus and he got the assignment.

Most other units had Pathfinders who received specialized training before being deployed to Vietnam, but the 25th was going to provide training in-country for the men selected. There were 13 enlisted men, along with Jim and one other officer (1st Lt. Tom Curran). They became the 25th Pathfinder Detachment, assigned to the 25th Aviation Brigade. They were all experienced soldiers, but none had previous Pathfinder training. They received an additional 10 days of orientation training for their assignment. Jim assisted with the training using some of his previous Ranger training and became the Assistant Commander for the detachment.[3]

Before a mission there was always an operational pre-plan. Careful coordination with all elements of the operation was crucial for success. Once the purpose of the mission was determined, including the size and scale, maps were consulted, call signs were given and other details were planned out as carefully as possible. Whenever possible, Jim would overfly the area ahead of time so he could see for himself what the area looked like. Often things didn't go as planned, but a plan was still vital.

Depending upon the mission and manpower availability, 1 to 4 men were inserted by helicopter to prepare the landing zones. A primary concern was enemy troops. Pathfinders avoided the enemy at all costs, since they had no heavy weapons should they get into a firefight. The whole idea was that they not be seen. Once they landed they were the eyes on the ground for the upcoming operation.

In order to confuse the enemy, the Huey helicopter that brought them might touch down at 3 or 4 places before the men got off in order to fool the enemy about their exact location. Sometimes they came into the area in a single helicopter and other times they had gunships with them. They varied their techniques.

The first priority was to reconnoiter the area in order to locate and avoid any enemy troops in the immediate area. After this they worked on the task at hand, locating the best possible location for the troops to land, noting such things as the height of the grass, which could be very misleading from the air. Hopefully they had chosen an area where the helicopters could get in and land without any obstructions.

Sometimes the enemy placed mines in open areas, anticipating the possibility that these areas could be used to land helicopters with troops. One type of mine was placed on a pole in long grass, with some kind of detonator on top that could be set off by a helicopter landing, so the areas had to be quickly and carefully checked out by the Pathfinders on the ground.

Aids for navigation would also be determined, such as the speed and direction of the winds, again for the incoming choppers. The Pathfinders determined the best direction for the approach. When the airborne assault actually took place the Pathfinders became Air Traffic Controllers, handling all instructions for pilots and crews, as well as giving advice to the pilots on the location of any incoming fire and other hazards.[4]

Pathfinders were in charge of the landing zones throughout the entire insertion operation. As long as troop-carrying Hueys (Slicks) were coming in, the Pathfinders controlled the landing zone. Artillery and equipment might be brought in immediately after the infantry. If equipment was needed, other Pathfinders would be back at the base camp, rigging the equipment to be slung beneath larger CH-47 Chinook helicopters and delivered to the LZ.[5]

Once the troops and their equipment were on the ground, in most cases the Pathfinders would board the last chopper and return to their base. The ground commander assumed full responsibility at that time. When it came time to evacuate the wounded or the men on the ground had completed their mission, Pathfinders could be brought in again to coordinate their extraction.

Night missions were particularly dangerous, for obvious reasons. Under Jim's leadership and the training of his Pathfinders, his detachment developed full night time air assault capability, something few other units had achieved in Vietnam in 1966. By the time Jim left to go home he had participated in more than 200 combat missions.[6]

Jim led the first ever night time airmobile assault by helicopter in his division in September 1966. It was as carefully planned as possible, but still, it had never been tried. He was assisted by four of his Pathfinders.

This wasn't a particularly large mission and the plan was for just one or two companies to land and participate. A large North Vietnamese Army (NVA) unit was believed to be in the region. The Americans would actually be working with South Vietnamese troops on this mission. The ARVN troops were already on the ground and trying to locate and engage the NVA. The ARVNs were to be the primary force, with the American troops assisting.

Surprise was of the essence and the place selected for the LZ was near several villages. Since it was in an area that was more populated than others they made the decision to go in shortly before bringing in the troops, less than an hour before the infantry was brought in. Hopefully the presence of the one Huey that brought them in wouldn't create too much attention.

The Huey appeared out of the darkness and began its descent. It descended quickly and hovered a few feet over a rice paddy. The five Pathfinders jumped out of the chopper into knee-deep water and the helicopter left as quickly as it appeared.

So far so good. When the chopper left they could see and hear tracer rounds in the distance. None of it appeared to be aimed directly at them, but the fire was in their general direction. Now in complete darkness, the men dispersed to complete their tasks. They knew their assignments and there was no need for talk. They placed small bean bags with lights attached on top of dikes around the paddies. The lights were low to the ground and could easily be seen from the air but were not clearly visible from the ground, at least not from a distance. Each light marked the designated landing site for a single helicopter.

Soon the Slicks were on the way and being directed to the LZ by one of the Pathfinders with a radio. The men heard the helicopters approaching as the radio operator directed them to the LZ. When the Hueys approached the LZ, the lights beneath them came into view.

Jim stood in the paddy with a flashlight in each hand to direct the helicopters. As two staggered trails of Slicks approached the makeshift LZ, for some unknown reason the pilot of the lead Huey turned on his landing lights, illuminating Jim and the area beneath the helicopter. A quick cautionary reminder from the Pathfinder on the radio resulted in the pilot immediately extinguishing the lights.

As the lead helicopter approached the LZ, Jim raised his arms high above him to get the pilot's attention and to let the pilot know he was now providing him with landing instructions. As the Slick came closer, he moved one arm to the side to let the pilot know he wanted him to move in that direction. When the helicopter was where he wanted it, he moved both outstretched arms down to instruct the pilot to descend. When the chopper was properly positioned, he lowered his arms further and crossed his arms, the signal for the pilot to land or to hover low enough for the troops to jump out.

This was accomplished and the lead helicopters and several others in the formation behind them set down, assisted by other Pathfinders with flashlights, and the infantrymen quickly jumped off. The Slicks immediately took off, leaving as directed by the Pathfinder with the radio. Other helicopters were already approaching. The off-loaded infantry moved away from the LZ to prepare for the mission, setting up a temporary perimeter in case they were attacked.

Jim met briefly with the ground commander, who was on one of the first helicopters to land, for a last minute debrief, then got ready for the next group of helicopters, once again providing hand signals for the lead Slick. Several waves of choppers had now dropped their troops at the LZ. Unlike in many cases where all the Pathfinders would board the last chopper leaving and return to their base, Jim sent three of them back to base and he and one other Pathfinder joined up with the infantrymen, just in case they were needed to coordinate a rapid extraction.[7]

On this mission there were no encounters with the enemy ground forces, but there was a bit of a show later that night. Off in the distance several miles away Jim saw and heard "Puff", always a welcome presence for the infantrymen. Puff was a twin-engine modified C-47 cargo plane of WWII vintage. It was equipped with three Gatling mini-guns, each capable of firing 2,000 rounds of ammunition per minute. A steady stream of light arced from the aircraft as Jim watched it making circling passes in the distance. It had obviously found a target to destroy.

They encountered no enemy that night and later the next day Jim and the other Pathfinder coordinated the extraction of the troops by helicopter from the area. He didn't learn the specifics of what occurred with the ARVN troops but thought it likely that Puff had destroyed the NVA force or at least scared them enough that they left the area. Puff was a powerful force. The Pathfinders had successfully completed their first night mission without any problems and continued to hone their skills on night missions that followed.[8]

Jim led many other Pathfinder missions the next few months. In December 1966 Jim was nearing the end of his tour. While at the 25th Division headquarters at Cu Chi, Bob Hope and his entourage arrived to perform on their Christmas tour. Jim was assigned to be one of Bob's escorts during the troupe's time at Cu Chi. It was

FIG 17 - JIM WITH BOB HOPE-DEC 1966

a nice opportunity for him to be able to meet Bob, but the highlight was when singer/dancer Joey Heatherton came up and gave him a big kiss after their performance. A couple of weeks later he was on his way home.[9]

Jim served the remainder of his time in Virginia. While still in the Army he went back to school, receiving a Masters of Commerce degree at the University of Richmond. He achieved the rank of captain by the time he was ready to leave the army in December 1969. He got a job with Xerox Corporation and moved to California in 1970.

After gaining experience with Xerox, Jim and a friend started a copy center business called Copymat in Berkeley, California in 1974. The business grew and they opened several other stores and the business became franchised a few years later. Jim broke off from Copymat in 1988, selling several of the stores he owned. He ventured into the mortgage business, becoming a mortgage broker and a loan officer. He is talking of retirement, but it's unlikely he'll ever retire completely.

Jim and his wife Deborah live in Danville, California. In addition to belonging to Viet Nam Veterans of Diablo Valley, Jim belongs to the VFW, the American Legion, the Disabled American Vets and the National Pathfinders Association.[10]

FIG 18 - JIM HILL TODAY

NOTES AND REFERENCES

[1] Although the operations inside Vietnam were not actual invasions, U.S. troops did invade Cambodia in 1970.

[2] There were three 81MM mortars and two 106MM recoilless rifles that made up the weaponry in the mortar platoon.

[3] Other Army units had Pathfinders, but most received training before they went overseas.

[4] Although the Pathfinder had the overall responsibility for the insertion, the pilots still had responsibility for their helicopter and crews. The Pathfinders were there in an advisory capacity.

[5] Common items delivered to the LZs were ammunition, artillery, water and food. All of this depended upon the size and length of the operation.

[6] Jim Hill's efficiency report provided the exact number of missions as 216. From U.S. Army Officer Efficiency Report, Form 67-5, dated 3/6/67 for 1st Lt. James Hill covering dates 6/3/66-1/3/67.

[7] Since this was not an extended mission, where additional equipment was needed, no additional helicopters were used to bring in equipment.

[8] Some of the details for the story of this night mission are from the 9/23/66 issue of Stars And Stripes, a story entitled "Pathfinders Show Way", written by SP4 Todd Darch.

[9] Joey Heatherton was a popular singer/dancer/actress in the 1960's and 1970's. She accompanied Bob Hope on several of his Christmas tours.

[10] The author interviewed Jim Hill for this story on 12/22/16, 3/28/17 and 4/10/17.

Chapter Three

A Jiffy Pop Christmas

SP4 (Specialist 4th class) Steve Mazaika found himself in the 4th Aviation Battalion of the 4th Infantry Division in the Central Highlands of South Vietnam in 1966. He arrived there in September, when his division deployed from Fort Lewis, Washington. His division didn't fly to Vietnam, as most other units did, but sailed there on three crowded troopships. It wasn't a pleasure trip, with the troops crowded inside the ships and their bunks piled high beneath the decks. He wasn't unhappy to get off the ship when they arrived in Vietnam in September of that year.

His base was Camp Enari, the division headquarters for the 4th Infantry Division. The actual airfield where he was stationed was called Hensel Airfield. He was assigned to fire and rescue at the airfield. In typical Army fashion, there were no fire trucks on his arrival. In fact, the fire trucks didn't arrive until nine months later, making it a little difficult to fight fires.[1]

The 4th Infantry Division's arrival came fairly early in the Vietnam War as the U.S. was building up its forces. Camp

Enari was near Pleiku, in the Central Highlands. A primary role for the division would be the interdiction of enemy forces from Cambodia. There wasn't much enemy action in this area when Steve arrived, but the enemy build-up had begun and would continue to increase during the year that he was there.

Steve is a native Californian and spent his youth in the small town of Lafayette, about 20 miles east of San Francisco. It was a small town, peaceful and quiet and somewhat rural in those days. Steve graduated from high school in 1961 and immediately got a job with the local fire department at age 17, initially to fill in when firefighters were on vacation. Four years later he was drafted into the U.S. Army in October 1965.[2] As a result of his previous firefighting experience he was trained as a firefighter before being deployed with his division to Vietnam.

FIG 19 - PVT. MAZAIKA IN TRAINING

Since there were no fire trucks on Steve's arrival he assumed other duties in his company. He drove a truck, carrying supplies. He helped with the construction around the field, including such things as pouring concrete, building an improvised shower for the men, and helping with the construction of various buildings. In addition, he and his firefighting buddies were required to be on standby at the airfield from the time that the helicopters assigned there took off on a combat mission until they landed, just in case there were any accidents or fires. They had a truck that could spray dry chemicals, but no actual fire truck. He kept busy with all of his other duties.

When the Christmas holidays came around, for some of his team it was their first Christmas away from home and for nearly all of them it was their first Christmas out of the United States. A few days before Christmas he and his buddies began receiving packages from home. It was great to get the gifts, but it was still a reminder they were away from their loved ones.

Steve and five of his buddies had an idea. They could see the poverty around them and decided to share their goodies and time on Christmas Day with the Montagnards in a small village of about 100 residents just a few miles from their base. The Montagnards had been given their name many years before by the French and meant "mountain people" or "mountain dwellers". This group was clearly a minority in Vietnam. They looked different than the Vietnamese if one looked closely and their language was different. They had

FIG 20 - SAM THE INTERPRETER

undergone persecution for years and lived in small villages in the Central Highlands of South Vietnam.

Steve and his friends saved the candy and food they received for Christmas and on Christmas Day, loaded the gifts into a ¾ ton truck and drove to the nearby village. The villagers were elated to see them and ran to greet the Americans. Fortunately, the soldiers had an interpreter in the village they could rely on to help them communicate, a Montagnard named "Sam". Some of these villagers worked on the base as unskilled labor. They were very pro-American.

FIG 21 - STEVE MAZAIKA'S FRIENDS WITH MONTAGNARDS

The soldiers began sharing their food and candy on their arrival and played with the village children. Steve received a container of Jiffy Pop from home, a favorite American snack consisting of popcorn kernels in an aluminum pan with an aluminum foil top. When the pan was placed on a stove the top expanded as the kernels popped. There were no stoves in this primitive village but there were fires.

FIG 22 - STEVE WITH HIS NEW FRIENDS

Steve took the container into one of the hooches, raised several feet off the ground. He held the container over an open fire inside, with the mother and two children watching him closely. As the kernels began to pop the top of the container expanded. The children watched in awe, their eyes growing larger, as the container expanded, getting bigger and bigger. When it finished expanding Steve removed the container from the fire. He walked outside where the group was waiting. When he tore the aluminum off the top, spilling popcorn, the children shrieked in amazement, retreating a few feet. Steve put a piece of popcorn in his mouth, demonstrating to the children that it was edible, and good. The children approached and sampled the popcorn. Soon they were all eating it and not a kernel was left. Steve had supplied the edible magic for the day.

The six men spent the rest of the afternoon in the village, distributing the food and candy, playing with the children and talking to the villagers with the assistance of their interpreter. All good things must come to an end though, and in the late afternoon they got in the truck and headed back to their base, having spread some good cheer to some people who didn't expect it. The young men discussed their day in the village as they drove back. They arrived before the base gates were closed for the day and before the tanks were driven to the gate to defend the base against any night attacks. It wasn't Steve's best Christmas, but it was certainly a memorable one, having spent the day spreading good will with some very appreciative people. He would never forget it.[3]

Months later the fire trucks arrived and the men actually had the equipment to fight fires. There were some fires during that time period, including the one caused by the accidental firing of a rocket by a helicopter on the ground. The rocket hit another helicopter that was parked nearby in the

FIG 23 - STEVE (ON RIGHT) AND HANK LENHART

maintenance yard, blowing it up, causing quite an explosion and fire. There were also fires in the mess hall and re-enlistment offices, as well as a fire caused by a malfunction with a flame thrower on an armored personnel carrier. They were all put out without loss of life.

In February, Steve was promoted to sergeant (E-5). With this promotion he became a crew chief in crash rescue in B Company, 4th Aviation Battalion. At the beginning of September 1967, his tour was finished and he returned home, getting released from the Army a few days later. Steve was glad to be home and out of the Army. He returned to the Fire Department in Moraga and worked there until 1999, credited with 38 years of service.

Steve and his wife, Donna, live in Moraga. They have two sons. He is a member of the Viet Nam Veterans of Diablo Valley and also belongs to other Veterans organizations including the 4th Infantry Division Association, the Veterans of Foreign Wars (VFW) in Lafayette, and the Vietnam Helicopters Crew Members Association (VHCMA).[4]

FIG 24 - STEVE MAZAIKA TODAY

NOTES AND REFERENCES

---

[1] Camp Enari was named after 1st Lt. Mark Enari, a platoon leader in Company A, 1st Battalion, 12th Infantry Regiment, 4th Infantry Division, who was killed by enemy fire on 12/2/66. Hensel Airfield was named in honor of WO1 Ernest V. Hensel Jr, an OH-23 helicopter pilot, 10th Cavalry, 4th Infantry Division, shot down on and killed on 2/17/67. The base and the airfield were named after Steve Mazaika arrived in Vietnam.

[2] The fire department was called Eastern Contra Costa Fire Dept. when he was hired, but changed their name to Moraga Fire Dept. four years later. Today they are called Moraga/Orinda Fire Dept.

[3] The author noted that Steve had several photos of the Christmas visit in his photo album, a clear indication of its importance to him.

[4] The author interviewed Steve for this story on 9/8/16.

Chapter Four

No Ash and Trash Mission

Dick Sperling was an Independence Day baby, born in Elmhurst, Illinois on the 4th of July 1942, the youngest of three children. Growing up in Mt. Prospect, he and his brother were fascinated with stories told to them by a neighbor, a WWII Vet. He couldn't have imagined that years later he would have his own stories to tell. When he graduated high school in Michigan he entered Western Michigan University and also joined the ROTC program. Upon graduation in 1965, he was commissioned a 2nd lieutenant in the artillery. What he really wanted to do was fly, so he applied for helicopter flight school. He was accepted and successfully completed the training as a Huey pilot. The vast majority of pilots were sent to Vietnam. He was no exception.

Dick found himself in the Central Highlands of Vietnam in 1967. Like other green pilots assigned to the 2nd platoon, 155th Assault Helicopter Company, he flew as copilot with other experienced pilots out of Ban Me Thuot, their home base, which was near the Cambodian border. They flew "slicks" or Huey helicopters configured to carry troops into battle. Finally, on March 16th, after two months flying as a copilot, he was deemed to have enough experience to command his own crew as 1st pilot. During this time period they were supporting the 4th Infantry Division in an operation code named "Operation Sam Houston". It was a search and destroy mission that lasted several months, tasked with intercepting North Vietnamese forces infiltrating this part of Vietnam from Cambodia.

FIG 25 - DICK SPERLING

Dick's first mission as aircraft commander was a scheduled "Ash and Trash" mission. These were missions to deliver food, water and ammunition to men in some of the forward, more isolated areas. The night before the mission Captain Barney Hancock, the platoon commander, met with Dick and told him he was ready to assume the responsibilities of an aircraft commander. Dick mentioned that he hadn't really been in "the thick of it" so to speak and Hancock said that would happen soon enough. Neither knew it would happen so soon.

He learned the details of the mission during briefing. All missions could be hazardous, but this one looked to be pretty simple, a good mission to get his feet wet as an aircraft commander. Dick went out to his assigned Huey and noted it was one of the older birds in the unit. It looked worn out with faded paint and sections of Plexiglas windows taped together, temporary repairs at best. Sperling decided to fly in the right seat for this mission, since this was where he flew most of his previous missions. Normally the copilot flew in this seat, but he liked it, particularly since there were more instruments and gauges on this side.[1]

The pilots didn't have a regular crew and flew with different crewmen on most missions. Today his copilot was Bill Christobal, a Warrant Officer (WO). The door gunner was SP4 Tom DeSimone and the crew chief was SP5 Mike Baucom. They weren't men he knew well, but they were good men, as the day would later prove.

FIG 26 - (L-R) CHRISTOBAL, DISIMONE, BAUCOM, SPERLING

The squadron helicopters took off to deliver the supplies to the combat troops in the field. Just a few minutes later they received an emergency recall to their base and the men

49

quickly headed back to the tent for another briefing. The briefing major seemed excited and there was an air of urgency of his voice. He reported that there were clear indications that the North Vietnamese Army (NVA) was amassing troops not far from Duc Co, in the Ia Drang Valley, possibly with a battalion-size force. The mission had quickly changed to a combat assault. Things changed just that quickly in Vietnam. The helicopters were to fly to Duc Co, a 10 or 15-minute flight, where they would pick up infantrymen from the 4th Infantry Division and take them to a landing zone (LZ) near where the enemy was spotted.[2]

They flew to Duc Co and picked up five infantrymen for the air assault. They took off again, flying in 3-aircraft elements in "V" formation and were in the second element. Altogether there were 12 helicopters involved. Dick's call sign was "Stagecoach 23". The other two helicopters in his element were flown by his squadron commander, Captain Barney Hancock and Warrant Officer Jerry Johns. They didn't fly directly to the LZ, but orbited a few miles away, while the softening up process was taking place as the LZ was being prepped for the landings. First came an air assault, with bombs being dropped in the forest surrounding the LZ. This was followed by an artillery barrage. This entire operation was controlled by an officer in a Command and Control (C&C) helicopter, hovering several thousand feet about them, out of the immediate danger zone. After the artillery stopped, Huey gunships came in, raking the area with machinegun fire and rockets. It didn't appear to Dick that anyone or anything could survive this barrage.

As the gunships moved out of the immediate area, the first 3-helicopter element of Hueys approached the LZ. Dick watched as they were met by murderous gunfire from the surrounding trees and couldn't believe the volume of tracers he saw as the first three Hueys pulled up, aborting their landing. Dick's element continued in, led by Captain Hancock. All three helicopters managed to land and off-load their troops. They successfully took off and returned to Duc Co for more troops while other helicopters delivered their human cargo through the withering fire. Dick's group landed, picked up the waiting troops and returned.

They approached the LZ at a different angle this time, hoping to avoid some of the fire. Tracer fire was coming from both sides of the thick forest around the LZ and there were explosions in the LZ from incoming rockets or mortars. Hancock landed a little short, forcing the two helicopters behind him to wait until he off-loaded his troops and took off. Hancock's helicopter slowly lifted off the ground, staggering, the hydraulics shot out by ground fire. The men in the other helicopters didn't know it at the time, but the crew chief was hit in the back by ground fire that struck him just beneath his armored vest, severely wounding him. Hancock nursed the severely-damaged helicopter back to Duc Co, landing on the medevac pad to get medical attention for the wounded crew chief, SP5 James Patterson. It was too late for Patterson, who died before they landed.[3]

As soon as Hancock's helicopter lifted off the ground Dick came in to land, with Warrant Officer Jerry Johns landing his Huey to his left. The helicopters were on the ground for a just a few seconds as the infantrymen leaped off, but it seemed like hours, as the troops ran for the cover of the trees or flattened themselves on the ground. The noise of the gunfire was deafening, mixing with the noises of the helicopter engines. Dick noted that most of the fire seemed to be coming from his left, in the tree line beyond Johns' helicopter, with Johns' helicopter shielding him from some of the deadly fire.

Both Hueys lifted off, the crews anxious to get away from the shooting. Just after take-off Sperling's copilot, Bill Christobal, told Dick to look off to his left where Dick saw a ball of flame resembling a blow torch coming from the exhaust of Johns' Huey. The door gunner, DeSimone had a better view of Johns' aircraft. DeSimone had been firing his M60 machinegun at the tree line beyond the LZ, trying to suppress some of the fire that was mostly aimed at the troops they had just offloaded. DeSimone watched as the door gunner now stood on the skid outside the aircraft to escape the flames and smoke which now enveloped the entire back of the helicopter.[4]

Stagecoach 23 was behind Johns' helicopter now, watching as the rotors slowed and it lost power, descending with flames still shooting out the rear. Just before hitting the trees, the bird turned to the left and flared up before it crashed on its right side into the thick forest, where the tallest trees reached 100' or higher. Tree branches, debris and rotors flew in all directions.

Dick immediately called the C&C helicopter to advise them of the downed helicopter. It didn't appear there were any survivors, but he circled the area just in case, telling his crew to watch for any sign of life. He was surprised to hear one of the crew say "one out". Soon the crew reported "two out" and then "three out". His men had seen three men jump from the burning helicopter. It seemed a miracle that anyone could have made it out of the flaming wreckage. The crashed

Huey was about ½ mile from the LZ and the LZ was surrounded by NVA troops.

Dick circled around again. As he did so, he spotted a very small clearing in the thick forest, about ¼ mile from the survivors, in the opposite direction of the LZ. The clearing was just slightly bigger than a Huey. His crew had seen the site also. Dick keyed the intercom, asking the crew what they thought. Almost in unison, the three men answered, "Yeah, let's do it." Dick radioed the C&C helicopter, told them there were three survivors on the downed bird and his crew was going to attempt a rescue.

He brought the helicopter in, just barely managing to set it down in the small clearing without clipping the surrounding trees. Dick told Christobal to keep the engines running and to leave if things got too hot. He told the other two crewmen, door gunner DeSimone and crew chief Baucom, to remove their M60 machineguns from their mounts and set up defensive positions near the Huey. DeSimone took a position about 20 yards in front of the helicopter with his M60 in his arms. Baucom did the same alongside the helicopter.

Sperling grabbed his M-16 rifle and armed with it and his .45 caliber pistol (carried in his shoulder holster), he headed into the forest. He had no radio, so there was no possibility of communicating with anyone once he left. As he ran into the trees he realized it wasn't smart to go it alone, so thought better of it and ran back to the helicopter, telling Baucom to come with him. He took off his helmet and removed his chicken plate (armored vest), tossing them back into the aircraft.

Baucom, armed with the heavy M60 and three bandoliers of ammunition, followed. As Dick ran into the forest again he looked back and saw that Baucom was weighed down with all the weight he was carrying and couldn't keep up, so he grabbed a couple of the bandoliers from Baucom and they ran into the forest together in the general direction of where the smoke was coming from. They could only see a few feet in front of them, due to the thick overgrowth, so they could only guess at the location, but several minutes later they reached the crash site. Dick hadn't noticed any direct fire as they went to the crash site, but there was a lot of shooting nearby and the enemy was certainly aware of the location of the downed helicopter.

Dick had spotted smoke and the downed aircraft through the trees. Johns and his copilot, Bill Schurr, were near the burning wreckage, standing over the wounded crew chief. The crew chief had a severe wound to his leg and the pilots had put a pressure bandage on the bleeding wound before the rescuers arrived. Dick learned from the men that the door gunner, Sgt. Keith Griffin, was dead and was still in the burning wreckage.

Dick told the men they needed to get out of there. Johns and Schurr wanted to try to recover weapons from the burning wreckage, but he told them they had to get out of there immediately, knowing the enemy wasn't far away and would soon find them. Dick and Baucom stood on each side of the wounded crew chief, his arms draped over their shoulders and they took off into the forest, followed by Johns and Schurr. Now there were some explosions in the trees near them, a clear indication that the enemy knew of their presence and was likely shooting mortars. This was confirmed when they heard the crack of a rifle. There was at least one sniper shooting at them and it wouldn't be long before NVA ground troops would be on them.

Suddenly there were thunderous explosions around them and they hit the ground. The men didn't know it at the time, but Christobal, back in the Huey, realized the NVA troops were closing in and called for an airstrike. The sounds were those of friendly A-1 Skyraiders, propeller-driven planes, providing close air support, shooting rockets and dropping bombs nearby. When the explosions subsided, the men got up and started moving again. At this point Dick was unsure of the location of the helicopter, unable to see anything through the thick foliage. He just kept the men moving and, after what seemed like an eternity, they heard the engine sounds of the waiting helicopter and saw it through the trees.

Johns and Schurr climbed aboard the helicopter. When DeSimone saw the men returning he ran to Baucom who was assisting the wounded man, picked up the wounded survivor and carried him to the helicopter. Dick was tired, but didn't realize the extent of his exhaustion as he climbed into the copilot's seat. When Christobal offered to fly the helicopter, Dick refused the offer. He managed to take off, but once airborne, his legs were rubbery and shaking. At this point he turned over the controls to Christobal.[5]

They flew back to the medevac pad at Duc Co, where medical staff brought out a stretcher and loaded the wounded crew chief onto it, carrying him away for treatment. The crew chief was moaning and in excruciating pain. As the crew stood by, exhausted, they took a close look at the Huey, walking around it. Miraculously, through all that fire, they had no new damage, not one single bullet hole. Unbelievable!

Dick turned on the radio to get an update on the situation. He reported in and was told more troops were needed on the ground at the LZ.

He couldn't believe it! After all that he and his crew had to go back again. They picked up five more infantrymen and took them to the LZ, expecting more murderous fire, but it was quiet when they arrived. There was no more firing from the tree line. The infantry had done their job. This was their final insertion that day and they headed home. It had been a mission that none of them would ever forget, but there would be many others, hundreds of them. Dick still believes there was another unseen crewman on his helicopter that day, watching over his crew.[6]

Late in 1967 Sperling returned home and remained on active duty for ten more months. He stayed in the Army Reserves, retiring as a full colonel after 30 years of active and reserve duty. During that time period he became a commercial pilot for United Airlines, ultimately retiring in 2002.

He has kept busy since his retirement by volunteering for the V.A. at the Veterans Hospital in Martinez and by his participation in charitable events sponsored by the Viet Nam Veterans of Diablo Valley, and he is also currently on the Board of Directors for Vietnam Helicopters. He belongs to the American Legion, the VFW and MOA (Military Officers Association). He is the past president of the Legion of Valor and serves as that organization's historian. Dick is an active participant and supporter of the Third Thursday Lunch Group, a local informal group of veterans started by several WWII Vets. He has served as an assistant scoutmaster for the Boy Scouts and is an active supporter of the Experimental

Aircraft Association Young Eagles program, encouraging young people to learn to fly. Dick and his wife, Marilyn, live in Pleasant Hill, California.[7]

FIG 27 - DICK SPERLING TODAY

NOTES AND REFERENCES

[1] As he gained more experience on later missions he switched to the left seat.

[2] The Ia Drang Valley was same the location where the actions depicted in the book *We Were Soldiers Once... and Young*, took place.

[3] The information about the circumstances of Patterson's fatal injuries came directly from Barney Hancock in an email dated 2/27/15. Hancock obtained another helicopter to continue the mission of delivering troops to the battlefield.

[4] DeSimone's statement was published in the *Ban Me Thuot Barb,* the newsletter for the 155th Helicopter Assault Association, in February 1999.

[5] Christobal later related to Sperling that the commander in the C&C helicopter advised him to take off and leave the area when waiting for the men to return, due to the nearby enemy activity, but Christobal refused.

[6] The After Action report for Operation Sam Houston for 3/16/67, reveals that the LZ that day was YA758368. Five U.S. soldiers were killed (including the two on the helicopters) and three were wounded. Two additional infantrymen were killed while engaging an NVA squad after the landing and five were wounded. The unit that conducted the combat assault was 1st Battalion, 12th Infantry.

[7] Other primary sources of information for this chapter were three interviews with Dick Sperling, on 2/19/15, 2/26/15, and 9/4/15, as well as *Official History of the 155th Helicopter Assault Company*, Operation Sam Houston After Action Report, 16 March 1967 and a newspaper story in the March 26, 1967 edition of Dragon News, a 52nd Combat Aviation Battalion publication. A summary of Dick's story is included in his Distinguished Service Cross Citation, U.S. Army, Vietnam, General Order 3212, July 6, 1968.

Chapter Five

11 Bravo and More

John "T.J." Trujillo was an infantryman, a rifleman, a grunt. The Army had classifications for every "career" specialty or Military Occupation Specialty, abbreviated to M.O.S. The classification for infantryman was 11B or phonetically, 11 Bravo. This certainly wasn't going to be his career. He was a grunt. He was a rifleman, so he carried an M-16 rifle, went on ambushes at night, search and destroy missions in the day, and was later on company-sized sweeps, looking for the Viet Cong in the Central Highlands of Vietnam.

FIG 28-T.J. TRUJILLO

The 19 year-old was drafted into the Army in August 1966. A Colorado native, he grew up in Pueblo, before moving to the San Francisco Bay Area after high school where he lived with an uncle and an aunt. It took him several months to find employment, then was drafted as he was settling into his job. That's the way it goes.

He had just turned 20 when he arrived in Vietnam in February 1967. After several days of waiting he was assigned to the 1st Cavalry Division, whose home base was in the Central Highlands of Vietnam at An Khe. The name of their base was Camp Radcliff. The 1st Cavalry Division was airmobile, using helicopters for transport instead of the horse-mounted cavalry of earlier times. T.J. was assigned to the 2nd Battalion, 7th Regiment, Colonel George Armstrong Custer's unit, the same unit Custer led when he and his men were wiped out at the Battle of the Little Big Horn in 1876. The 1st Cav had been in Vietnam for two years and T.J. came in as a replacement. He didn't spend much time at Camp Radcliff, but was soon assigned to his unit's area of operations at Phan Thiet, close to the South China Sea.

FIG 29 – T.J. TRUJILLO

After several months he was a seasoned combat Vet, having been "in-country" for more than seven months. His squad had been tested in skirmishes and battles several times and they grew to depend on each other. Their squad leader, a sergeant, certainly didn't lack courage, but had a problem keeping his arm down when a request was made for volunteers. The sergeant wasn't just volunteering himself, but the entire squad. Now he had done it again.

Things were nice and quiet that morning at Phan Thiet until the sergeant came and told the squad to "saddle up", that he volunteered for another assignment. The men quickly, but not happily, gathered their gear as the sergeant explained the mission. A low-flying reconnaissance helicopter was flying over Highway 1 and observed some fresh dirt mounds on the road, a sign the Viet Cong were mining the road. Highway 1 was the main road used to transport supplies and now the road couldn't be used until it was checked out and any mines cleared. Their assignment was to clear the mines.

T.J. and the others couldn't help but wonder why this man kept volunteering them as the 8-man squad took their helicopter ride up to the area where the potential mines had been spotted. Maybe he was hoping for a promotion, maybe he was trying to please or maybe he was just bored. His reason didn't make any difference. The men didn't balk at assignments, even dangerous ones, but they didn't appreciate all of this volunteering.

The helicopter landed in a clearing adjacent to a rice paddy alongside the road. Rice paddies stretched along the left side of the road, which was paved with asphalt in this area. The right side of the road was covered with vegetation, brush and trees. T.J. and the others got off and the helicopter lifted off, leaving the men to clear the road. T.J. could hear the sound of automatic weapons fire in the distance. It was at least a mile or two away. There were also other helicopters in the direction from which he heard the gunfire, so there must be some sort of a skirmish going on there. The 1st Cav must be engaged somewhere up there, but that wasn't of immediate concern.

One couldn't miss seeing the mounds of dirt on the road. The mounds were at least 2' high, dome-shaped, several feet apart on top of the asphalt. They clearly didn't belong there and had been placed the previous night. This was a well-traveled road and there was no way any vehicles could have driven around them yesterday. The men discussed how they were going to deal with this. There were at least 20 of these mounds. It was unlikely that each one contained an explosive charge, but each had to be checked out carefully. The VC would place mines inside the dirt mounds, hoping to blow up whoever attempted to disarm them.

Four of the men were assigned to perimeter security. They perceived the main threat would likely be from the right side of the road, among the trees where there were more places of concealment. They couldn't eliminate the possibility of a sniper in the rice paddies, so the four men assigned would also have to keep an eye on both sides of the road. The other four men, including T.J. and the sergeant, would check out the mounds. They would use their bayonets to probe. If they felt anything abnormal, such as something metallic, they would back off and call for someone with more experience to remove and/or detonate the mine. The men would have preferred that the guys with the mine detectors handle the whole operation, but for whatever reason T.J. and his buddies would have to handle it.

T.J. had a little training on mines, but very little. Experience in Vietnam taught him that sometimes the Vietcong would use an American mine as a booby trap. A weight would be placed on the mine and, once the weight was removed, the mine would detonate. The VC also used "Bouncing Betty" mines. These were very effective anti-personnel mines. He witnessed what these could do. A trip wire detonated a small charge, causing a larger charge to fly up and explode a few feet off the ground, sending shrapnel in all directions. He couldn't eliminate the possibility that there were other types of explosive devices of which they weren't even aware.

The four men assigned to this duty removed virtually all of the equipment they carried on their bodies, including their back packs and web belts. The only things they carried were their rifles and their bayonets and wore their steel helmets. They were never without their rifles, even though they would be crawling down the road.

The men got down on the pavement and began slowly crawling toward the mounds, watching for any strings or other objects attached that could be used to detonate an explosive charge. As T.J. approached the mound nearest him he was sweating profusely. He was always sweating in Vietnam with the high temperature and humidity, but today the sweat wasn't dripping, but pouring down his forehead, making it difficult to see. The hot asphalt didn't help matters and the entire front of his body was hot. His visual inspection revealed nothing protruding from the mound, so he probed into the dirt ever so carefully, first around the perimeter, then gradually sinking his bayonet deeper into the mound. It seemed to take forever, but he had to be careful. There would be no second chance if he didn't do it right. When he felt comfortable that there was no explosive device inside this mound, he crawled on to the next one and the next one. The sergeant and two other men were doing the same thing. It was very quiet. The men weren't talking, just focusing on the job at hand. The suspense increased each time they cleared a mound that didn't have a mine.

After more than an hour T.J. began probing around the perimeter of his fifth mound. He was really hot now, his clothes saturated with perspiration. Something about this one seemed different. As he probed a little deeper he felt something more solid. It didn't have a metallic feel, and there was no metal-to-metal sound, but it was solid. It certainly wasn't just dirt and it didn't feel like a rock. He backed off for just a second, thinking about what he should do next.

This wasn't a good situation. The sweat was really pouring down his forehead now. Couldn't Sarge have just kept his arm down this one time? A guy could get killed doing these things. Ever so carefully he pushed the bayonet further into the mound. He felt more resistance, and then it happened. The mound exploded, dirt flying in all directions. "Ahhhhhhhhhhhhhhhhhhhhhhhh!" was the deep, involuntary guttural sound that came from somewhere deep in his throat. He froze and just lay there, trying to catch his breath, his heart pounding. Is this how it would end for him? Was this how it felt to be dead? When he finally looked up he saw a huge bullfrog jumping away. He hadn't probed a mine, but had disturbed the temporary home of the frog! He didn't know who was more scared, he or the frog. When he got his bearings and recovered his composure his heart was still racing. He looked around and saw and heard his buddies laughing. It would take a while to live this one down.

The squad slowly and gingerly finished their task, checking each mound, without finding any explosive devices. This had just been an effective delaying action on the part of the VC. They had stopped travel on the road for several hours by making several dirt piles. Without further ado, the helicopter picked them up and flew them back to Phan Thiet. It had been just another day in the Nam, not really part of his job description as a rifleman, but one of these things that needed to be taken care of. T.J. wished all of the operations could have been this successful, with no losses. Unfortunately this was not the case.

FIG 30 – SQUAD LEADER TRUJILLO

T.J. completed his tour in Vietnam, spending the last couple of months as a squad leader toting an M60 machinegun. His tour ended just after the Tet Offensive began in 1968, and he flew home in early February. In August 1968, he left the Army and returned to California, to the San Francisco Bay Area. For several months he looked for a job, unsuccessfully, before landing a job at U.C. Berkeley, as a clerk in the Doe Library on campus. Meanwhile, he met and married his wife, Giulia. T.J. was at U.C. Berkeley when many of the demonstrations and riots occurred. Ultimately, he spent 40 years working for U.C.

Berkeley, the last eight years as a police technician at the U.C. Berkeley Police Department.[1]

FIG 31 - T.J. TRUJILLO TODAY

T.J. and his wife raised two children, have two grandchildren and live in Danville, California. He loves riding his Harley and participates in Warriors Watch Riders and the Combat Veterans Motorcycle Association. He is also active in AMVETS, where he is a district commander.

NOTES AND REFERENCES

---

[1] T.J. Trujillo was interviewed for this story on 10/26/15.

Chapter Six

A Short Tour

Gary Estrella was born in Honolulu, Hawaii. He spent his youth in Hawaii and in Concord, California, graduating from Mt. Diablo High School. Gary has one younger brother. After high school Gary went to Diablo Valley College in Pleasant Hill for two years. Even though Gary's brother was younger, he enlisted in the Marine Corps right after high school, while Gary was in college. A lot of young guys were being drafted and Gary decided to enlist in the Marine Corps, probably as a result of his brother's choice of service branch. Gary enlisted in the MARCAD program (Marine Cadet program) while still attending college, with the intention of becoming an officer, but that program was closed to civilian enlistees before he received a date to report for duty. As a result his enlistment contract was terminated.

There was a catch to his contract being terminated. Since he had enlisted under the MARCAD program and expected to report for duty, he hadn't applied for admission to a 4-year college. Consequently he lost his college deferment, subjecting him to the draft. If Gary enlisted in the Marine Corps, he could still apply for that program, so he enlisted. Catch 22 intervened again and the program was closed to enlisted personnel before he completed boot camp.

After boot camp he received radio telegraph training to become a radio operator. After completing this training he received orders for Vietnam. Gary arrived in Vietnam on August 10, 1967. It would be a short tour, although he didn't know it then, since most tours in the U.S.M.C. lasted 13 months. His tour ended on September 14th that same year. It wasn't an easy tour, but he survived.

FIG 32 – GARY AT BOOT CAMP GRADUATION

He didn't know much about his assignment, but knew he was going to the 3rd Marine Division in Vietnam. It was a long flight to Vietnam from the El Toro Marine base in California, with brief stops at L.A. International Airport, Hawaii, Wake Island, and Okinawa. There was a 2-day layover in Okinawa while the Marines got updated with inoculations before the final flight to Da Nang Airbase.

The heat and humidity struck Gary broadside as he walked down the stairs from the jet in the late afternoon. In typical military fashion a Marine from the base stood with a clipboard calling out names and unit assignments as the men got off the plane. "Estrella" was called out and Gary answered. He was told he was going to "2/9" and told to report to another sergeant. That Marine told him to report to a certain area on the tarmac and to wait for a plane that would be arriving to pick him up.

He waited for several hours and no plane arrived. An Army enlisted man was also waiting. As darkness fell he suggested they go get a bite to eat. They did and Gary returned after dark, and still there was no plane. There were no other Marines there going to 2/9. There was nothing to do but wait. He had his sea bag with his personal possessions and equipment so he laid down on the field with his head on the bag and made himself as comfortable as possible. There were two Army dog handlers and their dogs nearby, but he didn't want to get too close to them. The dogs looked pretty ferocious.

The next morning, after a restless and sleepless night for Gary, dayshift personnel started to arrive and, after another 3-hour wait, a C-123 transport aircraft arrived to pick him up. Gary and a few Vietnamese troops, who had arrived earlier in the morning, boarded the plane and they took off for the short flight to the Dong Ha Combat Base. Dong Ha was the closest village to the North Vietnamese border, less than seven miles from the DMZ (Demilitarized Zone). A jeep picked him up at the airfield and took him to H&S Company, his new home. Dong Ha was headquarters for the 9th Marine Regiment. Here he was issued his M-16 rifle and began to learn "the ropes". On the second day he experienced his first combat when he was inside the tent used as the living quarters for the communications platoon.

The tent was large with sandbags stacked 3' high around the base. He was in the tent when he heard a warning siren and then artillery shells and rockets began exploding around the base. Fortunately, none hit nearby but it was certainly a sign of what was to follow. These rockets and artillery were likely fired from somewhere north of the DMZ, so that's how close they were to North Vietnam. After a few days he realized the shells fell almost like clockwork around mealtimes. Usually there were just a few shells (3-4) fired, but occasionally there were more.

Gary's third day in Vietnam was interesting and a pleasant surprise when he learned of the 3:30 PM beer call. Some of his tent mates took him to a tent where they could obtain beer. It was warm, but it was still beer. It was also the day he went to the range and fired his M-16 for the first time, firing 200-300 rounds. He never fired an M-16 in the States, so this was a new experience for him, and an important one.

By this time he was assigned to radio watch, midnight to 2:00 AM, seven days a week. Patrols were sent out at night. Each patrol was required to send in a "Sit Rep" or Situation Report at regular intervals. Sometimes the radio operator just blew into his radio to answer the call, letting everyone know they were OK. It was fairly quiet this late at night. There were always two radio operators on duty in the bunker that contained the Combat Operations Center (COC), along with an officer in charge and an artillery officer.

Gary had a wakeup call a few days later. Behind the communications platoon tent was a makeshift shower. The structure itself was a frame made of 2x4 lumber, with canvas walls. On top of the roof was a 55-gallon drum filled with water that was heated by sunlight. This was their shower.

Gary was taking a shower when incoming shells began falling. He ran out of the shower to the bunker for safety. Inside the bunker was a Marine who had just returned from the hospital, having been wounded earlier. The Marine was yelling, "I'm gonna die! I'm gonna die!" The other Marines were trying to calm him, telling the hysterical Marine he wasn't going to die, but the Marine wouldn't listen, screaming "You don't know what you're talking about!" It was a sobering realization for Gary what war could do to someone. The Marine had completely fallen apart.

When shells started to fall the Marines all headed for bunkers, which were 6'X10' holes dug 3' into the ground. Sandbags were piled around the perimeter, with 4"-5" diameter logs piled on top of the sandbags, with more sand bags on top of the logs. They weren't comfortable, but they offered fair protection from incoming shells.

Several days later Gary's unit was told to prepare to move. It was to be his first and only operation in the field, "Operation Kingfisher". It was a Search and Destroy mission, aimed at blocking North Vietnamese forces entering Quang Tri Province from North Vietnam. In preparation for the mission Gary was issued a wooden pack frame for his radio, four pairs of sox, C Rations, 200 rounds of M-16 ammo and nine M-16 magazines, a cartridge belt, two canteens, six smoke grenades. [1]

They boarded trucks, enroute to the east side of Con Thien, very close to the DMZ. He was assigned as a radio operator to the A (Alpha) command group, led by a colonel. Within an hour or so they off-loaded from the trucks and set up camp. Gary had his poncho that he used as a tent and his "rubber lady" or air mattress to sleep on. They were at this location for just a couple of uneventful days and then moved down the road on foot, walking for about two hours, where they set up again.

Gary was assigned to 2-hour radio watches, monitoring the radio and checking on the ambush patrols that were sent out. On the night of September 12, 1967, it was very dark when Gary made his way back to his poncho after his 2-hour shift and tried to sleep. He had just fallen asleep when he was awakened by machinegun fire in the distance. Soon the word passed from other Marines that men were shooting at shadows and the fire died off and it became quiet again as the men tried to get back to sleep.

Just before dawn he was awakened again by mortar shells falling very close by. Gary heard a yell from the operations tent, a call for a radio operator. By this time he was running the 40 yards through the darkness to the command post, which was nothing more than a poncho propped up with sticks on four corners. He yelled "I'm here!" when he arrived, but there was already a radio operator there and he wasn't needed, so he began running back to his poncho and the hole he'd dug alongside it. There were mortar shells exploding all around him now as he zig-zagged through the darkness, feeling the adrenaline, his heart pounding.

As the mortar blasts marched closer to him, he dived to the ground, anticipating another explosion. Immediately a mortar shell exploded on the ground 15' behind him and to his right, showering the area with shrapnel. In the process his helmet flew off. He knew right away that he'd been hit, but he felt no pain. He reached for and found the helmet, lying nearby. While picking up his helmet he saw a piece of jagged metal protruding from his right hand. Still he felt no pain. He put the helmet on and was drenched with rain water. He had grabbed another Marine's helmet and the Marine had apparently been using it to catch rain water. At least he hoped it was rain water.

It was then, just as it was turning light, that he heard the screams around him, muffled by the sounds of exploding mortar shells. He was not the only one hit. He recognized a radio operator on the ground near him who was bleeding from a leg wound. Also lying on the ground was another Marine more seriously wounded. From training Gary recognized this man had a sucking chest wound and rolled him onto his side so he could breathe. His breathing was labored, but at least he was breathing. He tried to make the Marine as comfortable as possible as they waited for a corpsman.

There were moans and screams and calls for "Corpsman" all around him, as injured and dead Marines lay on the battlefield. The responses by the corpsmen were quick as the mortar fire trailed off. The most seriously wounded, like the Marine with the chest wound, were treated first and quickly carried off on stretchers for helicopter evacuation. Even the commanding officer, Lt. Colonel Kent, was wounded.[2]

Still Gary felt no pain as he waited for the most seriously wounded to be evacuated. A later assessment would reveal that, in addition to the major right hand wound, there were more than 50 pieces of shrapnel in his hand, as well as shrapnel in his right wrist and forearm. He also had a more serious shrapnel wound in his right foot and additional shrapnel in his left buttocks, but still he still felt no pain as he watched Marines being carried off on stretchers.

When things had calmed down a bit and the more seriously wounded had been taken to the LZ, Gary began hobbling over to the landing zone, using his rifle as a crutch and being assisted by another Marine, Michael Dupaz. It took them several minutes to get to the clearing. He climbed onto the skid of a Medevac Huey and grabbed onto the support. There were two other wounded on the chopper with him, one ambulatory Marine and another on a stretcher. He sat down, resting on one butt cheek inside the helicopter, knowing he was wounded on the other cheek, but he still felt no pain. The Huey took off and minutes later they were at Dong Ha Combat Base.[3]

The Marine on the stretcher was taken off the helicopter at Delta Medical Evacuation Hospital. Gary tried to stand up and fell out of the chopper. His right leg didn't work! Obviously that injury to his foot was more serious than he thought. He was lifted onto a stretcher and the stretcher was lifted onto two sawhorses. He looked around and saw 20-30 Marines on stretchers in long rows beside him. His wounds were dressed.

From here he was loaded aboard a field ambulance, still on his stretcher. The stretchers were in vertical rows along both sides of the ambulance. As they drove the short distance to the main runway Gary's right leg hit the roof of the ambulance. There was immediate excruciating pain. He was lifted out of the ambulance by two stretcher bearers and loaded onto an awaiting plane. He was writhing in pain by this time. The doctor on the plane heard him, came over and gave him an injection, ½ of it in his left hand and ½ of it in his left thigh. This did the trick and he drifted off into a drug-induced sleep and woke up several hours later, lying in a hospital corridor on a stretcher. A clock told him it was 9:00 PM. Someone told him he was going into surgery and he drifted off again. Sometime later he awakened with pain in his foot, arm, and wrist. Until then he hadn't realized that he also had shrapnel wounds in his wrist. He was now in a hospital room and soon learned it was the Da Nang hospital.

Later that next day a Marine officer came into his room and told him he needed to shave. Now he knew he was still a Marine. He told the officer he was right-handed and there was no way he could shave himself with his wounds. The officer ordered him to get someone else to shave him and walked out. The Marine who was wounded with him, the one whom he'd seen with the leg wound, was in the same room with him. He asked this Marine to shave him.

The following day Gary was again loaded onto a plane and this time it was a longer flight, to the hospital at Clark Air Force Base in the Philippines. In this hospital, tubes were placed in his hand, foot and butt cheek to drain the fluids. He was put in a hospital room with three other severely wounded Marines. More shrapnel was removed from various places, but the wounds were left open to heal.

A week later he was flown to the U.S. Naval Hospital in Guam. Here he would have two more surgeries. Doctors there decided to leave the shrapnel in his foot, for fear of crippling him if they tried to remove it. They determined he had severe nerve damage to his right hand and told him he wouldn't be returning to combat in Vietnam, but would be going home. He was soon able to hobble around, first on crutches and then with a cane during the several weeks he was in Guam.

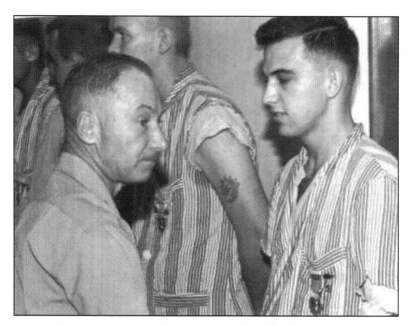

Fig. 33 – GARY MEETING WITH LT. GENERAL KRULAK WHILE IN THE HOSPITAL

On November 10, 1967, Gary arrived home, landing at Travis Air Force base in California. He phoned home as soon as he arrived. He and several other ambulatory patients were put on a Navy bus and taken to Oak Knoll Naval Hospital in Oakland. While being checked in by a doctor and medical staff, he was told that his mother and his fiancé were waiting for him in another room. When he finished checking in about 10 PM, the staff allowed him to spend an hour with his visitors. Needless to say, it was great to be home.

Gary was walking with a cane and could get around reasonably well, although he still needed treatment. One day he reported to the Marine Liaison Office to check on the status of his personal effects that he had left in Vietnam. The Officer in Charge examined his personnel file and noticed in his file a notation that he could type. The Marine corporal who held the position of Unit Diary Clerk had left and one of the primary requirements was the ability to type, so Gary was offered the job on a temporary basis. Bored with having little to occupy his time, he accepted.

His duties included such things as delivering pay to some of the hospitalized Marines, dealing with requests from families when Marines weren't writing home regularly, recording Marine intakes and discharges and other miscellaneous things he was asked to do. One assignment he didn't like was going to the morgue and measuring a dead Marine for a dress blue uniform for burial. The Marine was not killed in combat but died as a result of injuries from a bar fight.

He was allowed to go home on Christmas, a wonderful event and on December 30, 1967, he married his wife, Marcia. When he returned he was transferred to Casual Company at Treasure Island, awaiting reassignment. While at Oak Knoll he had seen some terribly injured Marines, which served as a stark reminder to him of how fortunate he was, despite his own serious injuries. Even though he was now at Treasure Island, he continued his temporary duties at Oak Knoll as the Unit Diary Clerk.

Gary was in and out of the hospital for ongoing treatment of his injuries. Since the injuries were obviously permanent he decided to apply for enrollment at California State College, Hayward several months in advance, expecting to be discharged. To his surprise, this was not to be. A Navy doctor told him he was fit for duty and was being returned to full duty, with a "profile on" his right hand and foot. This meant there were a few limitations and he was excluded from the rifle range and from combat drills.

The return to duty was a big surprise to Gary. He was still in pain, sometimes limping, and his foot continued to swell. This made no difference to the doctor and he was ordered to report to the Marine base at 29 Palms, California. The fact that he couldn't shoot a weapon with the nerve damage to his hand and couldn't march because of his foot injury was seemingly of no concern to the doctor.

29 Palms was a training base for desert warfare, a gunnery range and the headquarters for Fleet Marine Force Pacific. Gary worked in the ordnance office. In March of 1969 he was at work when he received a letter from the college in Hayward. It was his acceptance letter, giving him an enrollment date at the beginning of April. He chuckled, thinking of the irony of it all. The ordnance officer overheard him and asked him what he was laughing about. Gary explained the situation to him. The ordnance officer suggested he immediately complete the paperwork for an early discharge and said he'd approve it. Gary completed the application, the officer kept his word and Gary was discharged on March 23, 1969. A week later he started school.

Gary completed his Bachelor's Degree and started working. He later returned to school, John F. Kennedy University and obtained an MBA. Gary worked in marketing and contracting for 40 years, for various companies. The last place he worked was A.C. Transit.

He is now semi-retired and he and Marcia live in Danville, California. They have two children and five grandchildren. Gary is an active member of Viet Nam Veterans of Diablo Valley, a charter member of the Marine Corps League Detachment 942, a Life member of Disabled American Veterans, a Life member of the Military Order of

Purple Heart, and American Legion Post 246 member. He is also active in scouting and is the District Commissioner in the local council.[4]

FIG 34 – GARY ESTRELLA TODAY

NOTES AND REFERENCES

[1] He was actually issued four fragmentation grenades and two smoke grenades, but preferred the smoke grenades and exchanged the fragmentation grenades for smoke grenades.

[2] The USMC Combat Chronology for the 2nd Battalion 9th Marine Regiment indicates that 31 Marines were killed during the month of September and 239 were wounded, all a direct result of enemy action.

[3] Strangely enough Michael Dupaz's name was the only one he recalled from his entire Vietnam experience.

[4] The author interviewed Gary Estrella for this story on April 25, 2016 and on September 16, 2016.

Chapter Seven

Halloween Ambush

Fred Granados didn't begin his Vietnam tour as a combat medic in the U.S. Army, but that's how he finished it. He was trained as a dental lab technician, but the Army has a way of changing things around to suit its needs. No one could have guessed that he would or could be assigned to a combat infantry unit as a medic, with no specialized training.

Fred was born in Stockton, California, the son of a railroad man. He grew up with his older brother and sister, living first in Danville and then in other small towns in the San Francisco Bay Area. He attended high school in Concord, graduating from Mt. Diablo High in 1963. He enrolled at Diablo Valley College, with the dream of eventually becoming an orthodontist. To further this end he worked for an orthodontist part-time, fabricating orthodontic appliances. Soon he was doing this for several local dentists.

In order to maintain a student deferment from the draft in those days one had to carry what was known as a "full load" or 15 semester units and maintain a 2.0 or "C" average.

For one semester Fred maintained only 12 units, since he worked part-time. That was all it took to lose his student or 2S deferment and his status changed to 1A in draft parlance, throwing him into the pool of young men eligible for the draft. It didn't take long for the Army to find him and on May 5, 1966, Fred was drafted into the Army.

Fred wanted to be an infantryman, but when the Army learned he had worked for an orthodontist part-time while attending college they decided he should be a dental lab technician. After basic training he wasn't sent to advanced

FIG 35 – SP4 FRED GRANADOS

infantry training (AIT), but was sent instead to Fort Riley, Kansas where the 9th Infantry Division was being reactivated. He spent most of his time there setting up and taking down temporary field hospitals. In November 1966, the entire 9th Infantry Division was deployed to Vietnam aboard five ships. Fred's ship was the U.S.S. Upshur, a Korean War-era troop ship. The trip was long and boring.

The ships arrived at the port at Vung Tau, Vietnam. Vung Tau is the southernmost port city and is also the entrance to the Mekong Delta. Its population grew dramatically with the arrival of American troops. Due to a stevedore strike, the men remained on their ships for five days in the harbor, before they were transferred from the troopships to LST's (Landing Ship Tanks), which took them ashore. A big deal was made of their arrival. They were met by news teams, a band, and

General Westmoreland, who was on hand to greet the troops. Westmoreland commanded all troops in Vietnam.

They boarded trucks for their ride to Bearcat, the base where 9th Infantry Division headquarters was set up. The base was several miles east of Saigon in III Corps, not far from Bien Hoa. The 9th Division was tasked with defending the Mekong Delta region and keeping insurgents out of the area. Fred was assigned to A company of the 9th Medical Battalion, which operated the battalion hospital there, but he had no role as a dental technician. Those assignments were filled by others. Instead he was assigned to menial tasks around the base, things like K.P. duty, cleaning up trash and burning human waste that accumulated at the outhouses. He hated this assignment.

Two months later Fred learned that a doctor in Headquarters Company, a colonel, needed a driver. Nothing could be worse than being a trash collector, so he applied for the job. He was selected, without knowing the colonel was one of those spit and polish officers, requiring him to keep his uniform pressed and spotless and the jeep clean, washed and waxed. Still, it was better than burning human waste and picking up trash.

When he wasn't driving the colonel around, he spent his leisure time hanging around the division dental office, visiting with dentists and staff, interested in learning things that would be useful in helping him attain his goal of becoming an orthodontist. On a couple of occasions he even cleaned teeth, under supervision, of course.

Since this base was the division headquarters, here is where replacement infantrymen began their stint in Vietnam, becoming acclimated to being in a war zone. These new and inexperienced combat troops were often sent on a night ambush patrol near the base. They would leave the base on foot to an objective a half mile or so from the base in the late afternoon. The jungle was so dense that they would have to use machetes to hack their way through the growth. With an experienced non-com they would set up an ambush, with relatively little chance of encountering the enemy. It was a good training exercise.

Each of these ambush patrols needed a medic to accompany them. Some of the rear echelon headquarters medics weren't too interested in spending a night in the bush, so additional medics were often needed on these missions. Even though he wasn't a medic and had no medical training, Fred volunteered to fill in. Surprisingly enough, the powers that be allowed this. Fred went on several of these platoon-sized missions. Aside from the first patrol, when they received hostile fire, the missions were uneventful and his services as a medic weren't needed. After each mission he got the following day off, giving him a brief respite from the colonel and his shiny jeep.

Occasionally there were other breaks from his driving duties. There were MEDCAP excursions to the small nearby villages. MEDCAP stood for Medical Civilian Assistance Program. About once a week three doctors, accompanied by seven infantryman, would convoy out to a nearby village to provide medical treatment to the residents for illnesses, infections and diseases like malaria and pneumonia. They also gave injections. Fred was one of the seven men who went on several of these missions to provide security for the doctors, since no place was safe in Vietnam.

During other breaks from his chauffeur duties Fred hung around the field hospital. He watched as the wounded were brought in, observing the emergency treatment they received. The most seriously wounded were brought there for life-saving treatment before being transferred to a larger hospital. Those with less serious injuries were also treated. Fred got to know one of the sergeants at this hospital, who showed him how to suture wounds and eventually allowed him to suture some of the wounded, under close supervision. Fred also helped with the treatment of other injured soldiers, giving pain injections, cleaning wounds, assisting with triage, curettage and helping unload the helicopters when the wounded arrived.

Time passed and Fred's dislike of his assignment as the colonel's driver grew. This wasn't why he came to Vietnam. One day all the enlisted medical personnel were called together by the 1st Sergeant. He told them that three combat medics had been killed or wounded the previous day and replacements were needed immediately in the field. There would be a lottery later in the day and three men would be selected from the pool of medics to join these combat units.

Fred went back to his hooch with two of his bunkmates. These two medics had just arrived in Vietnam the previous week. One told Fred he was going to volunteer for the assignment. He left and returned several minutes later, saying he was accepted, leaving two open spots. Even though he wasn't a medic, Fred decided to volunteer. He had no formal training, but had assisted doctors and medical personnel on several occasions. He went to the first sergeant and volunteered. To his surprise, he was immediately accepted. With the stroke of a pen his classification was changed to combat medic. At that point the other medic in their hooch also volunteered and was accepted.

The next morning at 7 AM all three men were aboard a helicopter, headed south to join the combat units. Fred was assigned to a rifle platoon in B (Bravo) Company, 2nd Battalion, 60th Infantry, 9th Infantry Division. There were 19 men in this platoon, led by a lieutenant. A platoon was normally much larger, but had suffered many recent combat losses. Their previous medic, killed within the past couple of days, was well-loved and Fred had some large boots to fill. It didn't take long for him to be tested.

FIG 35A—FRED'S PLATOON. FRED IS IN THE FRONT ROW, 2ND FROM RIGHT.

In his new assignment Fred was both a rifleman and a medic. All hands were needed, especially since his platoon had so few men, resulting from earlier casualties and a lack of replacements. On his first mission he carried just a .45 caliber semi-automatic pistol as a weapon, along with his medical bag. He realized the pistol was of little or no use, so after that he carried (and used) an M-16. He had dual duties, to save lives and to take lives, if needed.

Fred carried very little in his medical bag. He asked each man in the platoon to carry bandages in a specific pocket, so that Fred could easily access the bandage if he came to the aid of that soldier. Among the items Fred carried were clamps, compression bandages, scissors, tourniquets, band aids, several syrettes of morphine and pint canisters of a blood-expanding liquid that he could use for a transfusion when a soldier had been wounded with severe blood loss. His role was supplying only emergency, life-saving first aid. The seriously wounded were taken out of the battle zone by helicopter as soon as possible (ASAP).

The platoon had two primary roles. They conducted Search and Destroy missions during the daytime and ambushes at night. Since this was the Mekong Delta, with its numerous waterways, they were sometimes transported by boat on closer missions and dropped off somewhere along the shoreline to search for the Viet Cong in a specific area. At the end of the mission they were picked up by boat again and taken back to their camp. On the more common missions farther from their base camp, they would be ferried by helicopter to the drop zone. These were known as Eagle Flights. If it was a "hot" landing zone and they received hostile fire, it would be a busy day. These missions could be just one day or could last several weeks.

The ambush missions were night missions. In fact, the platoon waited until dark before they left camp so as not to be seen. They would walk a distance and then set up for an ambush. The 19 men in the platoon would set up in a basic L-shape, spaced a few feet apart from each other.

Two or three claymore mines would be set up several yards in front of the formation. Lines with triggers to detonate the mines were run back to the men in the formation. Sometimes, after an hour or two with no enemy contact, they would move to another site and set up.

There were three men in the platoon who carried M60 machineguns. They were usually set up in each section of the "L", with the third man towards the center. Two other men who carried M-16 rifles also had starlight scopes, which enabled them to see through the darkness.

FIG 36 - FRED WITH TWO VC SOLDIERS HE CAPTURED ON A SEARCH AND DESTROY MISSION

One man carried an M79 grenade launcher. The grenade launcher had a stock and was fired from the shoulder. It resembles a single-barrel, large bore shotgun and it could fire a variety of different types of 40 mm grenades and was said to have a maximum range of 400+ yards, with a much shorter effective range. The man with the grenade launcher also carried a flare gun, useful in lighting up an area at night. The others in the platoon routinely carried M-16 rifles.

October 31, 1967, Halloween, was one such night operation, from their base camp at Tan Tru. The men assembled and waited until well after dark and then walked out of camp, as quietly as possible. It was nearly impossible to see through the darkness on this night, so their platoon leader made a decision to stay on a dirt trail near the village of Ap Binh Hoa. This wasn't an easy choice, because this left them vulnerable to an ambush and their role could easily change from hunter to hunted. The other choice was to stumble through the darkness, making noise and running into bushes and trees. So the platoon leader chose the trail. They had walked for about two hours to a spot which was about 2 ½ miles from their base camp.

It was about midnight when they came to this spot, which the lieutenant liked and they moved a few feet off the trail. There was a dike beyond them and the dike formed the outside edge of a rice paddy. The dike, about 3' high, offered them some cover if they stayed low. The rice paddy was flat, covered by a foot of water. With the concealment and protection offered by the dike, they had a clear field of fire across the rice paddy, should the VC approach from this direction.

The men set up quickly and quietly, whispering only when communication was necessary. They had done this many times before, so there was little need to talk. The three men with the claymores took them past the dike about 10 yards and set them up to point away from their position, spaced several feet apart across their perimeter, attaching the detonator cord and stringing it back to their positions. Soon they were in position, making sure that one of the men with the starlight scope was on each side of the "L"and that one of the men with the claymore detonator was alongside each infantryman with a scope. The entire length of the ambush perimeter was about 60', with the men spaced about 3' apart. Now came the difficult part...waiting.

FIG 37 - M79 GRENADIER "DAN" AND FRED GRANADOS

The men relied on the observers with the starlight scopes to let them know if the enemy was out there. If the enemy was spotted by one of the men with scopes the word came down the line in muted whispers. They had been set up for a while when word was passed down the line to Fred that VC were in the paddy, approaching.

The soldiers with the scopes waited for the enemy soldiers to get closer and they approached slowly through the paddy, unaware of the close proximity of the Americans. Soon they were within range. One man with a scope reached over and tapped the helmet of the soldier alongside him handling the claymore, the signal to detonate the mine. Almost immediately the other infantrymen detonated their mines. Automatic weapons fire broke out from both sides, reaching an ear- splitting, tornado-like roar of combat as both sides fired through the darkness. Fred fired along with the rest of the men, not being able to see a clear target. The automatic fire was punctuated by the detonations of 40 MM grenades as the soldier with the M79 did his job.

Fred soon heard a yell above the fire from the M60 machine gunner at one end of the line. "Doc, we gotta move the gun. You gotta protect us!" He quickly assessed the situation. The VC were trying to get around the end of the ambush site, trying to maneuver behind them to the trail, trying to turn the ambush around on the Americans. The gunner wanted Fred to draw the enemy fire away from the machinegun so the machine gunner and his ammo bearer could withdraw to a more advantageous position and keep the VC from getting behind them.

Without further thought, Fred grabbed the M-16 from the ammo bearer so that he would have two rifles. The VC had an advantage with their AK-47's in that they had a 40-round clip. He only had 18- rounds in his clips for the M-16's, so he wanted all the firepower he could carry. The second rifle allowed him to fire more rounds without changing clips.[1]

He crouched behind the dike and yelled at Dan, the grenadier, to fire a flare to light up the area. Fred heard the "poof" as the round left the flare gun and he jumped over the dike, running towards the VC, firing one of the M-16's on automatic as he sloshed through the water. As the flare lit the area for a few seconds Fred saw several VC running toward him. Seeing him firing, they turned and ran in the opposite direction. He ran about 20 yards after them, then stopped firing long enough to grab one of the grenades he was carrying, dropping down on one knee in the water. He quickly pulled the pin and threw it in the direction of the nearest VC soldier, who was running away from him.

After he threw the grenade Fred threw himself face down in the mud. His aim was better than planned and the grenade hit the VC in the neck, then exploded. The enemy fire was now directed at Fred and he lay in the water, making himself as small as possible as some of the VC fired in his direction, some of the rounds splashing in the water.

Meanwhile, the M60 gunner and the ammo bearer made it back to the trail and their fire kept the VC from outflanking them. When the fire had died down he ran back to the dike, jumping over it. The firefight continued for several minutes, with Fred making his way to both ends of the ambush site to check for wounded, firing over the dike at the enemy as he did so.

FIG 38 - A HAPPY FRED THREE DAYS BEFORE HIS TOUR ENDED

Several minutes later the firing died off and it became quiet again. As suddenly as it started, it was over. Fortunately, none of the Americans were wounded. Often on ambush patrol the platoon would move to another sight after a couple of hours, but on this night they stayed in their position, returning to their base camp at first light. They had seen enough action for one night. It was a heck of a way to spend Halloween.[2]

Fred completed his tour in early January, remaining in the field with his platoon until three days before the end of his tour. Some of the other missions weren't as successful and Fred's talents were often needed to treat the wounded. He was released from the Army to return to civilian life in May 1968.

Fred returned to Diablo Valley College upon his release from the Army, still hoping to become an orthodontist. A few months later he transferred to Sacramento State College to complete his Bachelor's degree in Biological Science.

Life has a habit of getting in the way of some of the best laid plans. After his release from the Army he had also taken a job with Southern Pacific Railroad. He stayed with the railroad for 20 years, even after obtaining his degree. After retiring from the railroad he became a licensed, independent insurance agent and eventually became a Professional Financial Planner, which he is still doing today. Fred is single and lives in Concord, California. He is an active member of Viet Nam Veterans of Diablo Valley.[3]

FIG 39 - FRED GRANADOS TODAY

NOTES AND REFERENCES

[1] The M-16 actually had a 20-round magazine or clip, but the rifle had a tendency to jam with a full magazine. Combat experience showed the tendency to jam lessened when only 18-rounds were carried in the magazine. This, along

with a stronger spring in the magazines, helped alleviate the jamming problem somewhat. The AK-47, with one type of banana clip, could carry 40 rounds. The 40-round clip was what Fred and his buddies usually confronted.

[2] 9th Infantry Division General Order #735, award of the Army Commendation Medal for heroism, dated February 9, 1968, provides a summary of the Halloween combat action. The order is for Specialist 4 Frederick Granados and references his assignment as "Medical Aidman".

[3] The author interviewed Fred Granados for this story on Sept 30, 2016, on October 23, 2016, on November 8, 2016 and December 23, 2016.

Chapter Eight

SEAL Team in Trouble...Scramble One!

They called him Moose. He was a big, strong guy. Occasionally he came over to the Officer's Club to have a few drinks with the Navy Huey gunship pilots at the Dong Tam base, located in the Mekong Delta. Dong Tam was the home of the 9th Infantry Division and the Riverine Assault Force, a joint Army/Navy force also based there. The gunship pilots were part of a separate force, "Operation Game Warden", which included the gunships, Navy river patrol boats, PACV's (Patrol Air Cushioned vehicle or hovercraft) and SEALs. Moose was a friendly enough guy for a SEAL team commander. Moose's base at that time was just a few miles away at My Tho.

On this particular evening, sometime in December 1967, Moose had quite a bit to drink. One of the chopper pilots asked Moose if he knew where the next mission would take his team. Moose pulled a map out of his back pocket and spread it on the table. The pilots watched as Moose covered his eyes with one hand, circling his hand over the map with his other hand, finally pointing at a spot near the center of the map. Ensign Ray La Rochelle, one of the pilots, saw that Moose's finger had landed on a place called Coconut Groves. This was right in the heart of "Indian Country", enemy territory, and there was no way even the SEALs would be going there on a mission. Ray was wrong. Two days later the SEAL team was inserted by river boat in the Coconut Groves area.

The Navy had a 2-gunship detachment of Hueys at Dong Tam, one of seven detachments placed strategically throughout the Mekong Delta. Ray La Rochelle was one of these pilots at Dong Tam.

FIG 40 - RAY LA ROCHELLE AT ENLISTMENT

Ray grew up in Northbridge, Massachusetts with two older brothers and two younger sisters. After high school he attended Worcester Junior College for one year before transferring to Northeastern University for his second year. It was 1965 and he saw the draft coming. Not wanting to be drafted he applied for and was accepted into the Naval Aviation Cadet (NAVCAD) program. By November of that year he was in the Navy, training to be a pilot. His flight training took 18 months and by the end of July of 1967 he was a Huey gunship pilot in Vietnam, in HA(L)-3, the Seawolves.

The gunships were on alert around the clock. The pilots and crewmen worked 24-hour shifts, 24 hours on and 24 hours off. When Ray first arrived in Vietnam at the end of

July, along with about 20 other pilots, the squadron was still forming and was awaiting delivery of the rest of their aircraft from the Army. Having no aircraft for them to fly, the skipper sent them all to Soc Trang to fly Combat Assault missions with the Army's 336th Aviation Company. Over the next 30 days Ray flew troop carrying missions with the army before rejoining his squadron at the end of August at Dong Tam.

When the unit arrived at Dong Tam, Ray and his buddies stayed in hooches about six blocks from the flight line. Since they were a quick response unit, the distance from the flight line caused a delay. A delay of just a couple of minutes could mean the difference between life and death for the men in the field. In order to respond more quickly, they brought in two small house trailers, (about 20 ft. long each), and covered them with sand-filled ammo boxes over a wood beam frame. This gave the crew protection from the frequent enemy mortar attacks on the base while situating them less than 50 ft. from their parked aircraft on their duty day.

FIG 41 - RAY LA ROCHELLE WITH HUEY GUNSHIP

On their duty days they lived in the trailers, the officer pilots in one trailer and the enlisted gunners and crew chiefs in the other. A radio was kept in the officers' trailer so they could monitor calls for assistance. Two UH-1B Huey gunships made up the detachment at Dong Tam. The helicopters were each armed with four forward firing M60 machineguns, two on each side of the aircraft. In addition there was one hand held M60 machinegun on either side of the cabin operated by the two door gunners. There were also two forward-firing rocket pods, each containing seven 2.75" rockets. They carried 8,000 rounds of M60 ammunition.

Fig 42 - HA(L)-3 Seawolves with armament

The detachment prided themselves on being able to be in the air within 60 seconds of receiving an emergency call for assistance. This was accomplished by the helicopters being prepped for the flight ahead of time. All of the switches were left on, except for the battery switch. The manner in which they operated certainly would not comply with FAA regulations, but this was wartime. They were always over their maximum gross weight on every combat mission.

The emergency calls for assistance were called "Scrambles" and there were three separate categories. The calls for assistance would normally come from the PBR's (patrol river boats) or from SEALs. In addition, they occasionally supported elements of the 9th Infantry Division, which was also operating out of the Mekong Delta. "Scramble 3" was the lowest priority, meaning that whomever made the call was in contact with the enemy and could use some help. "Scramble 2" meant that things on the ground weren't looking good and to speed up the response. "Scramble 1" was the highest priority call, a true emergency and a call for immediate assistance. The crews received regular calls for assistance. When a SEAL team called for assistance it was almost always "Scramble 1" and the call was always a whisper, sometimes barely audible. This was because, due to the nature of the SEAL team missions, they were always severely outnumbered and they normally didn't call for help unless it was a dire emergency. It was a whispered call because the enemy was so close to the team that a normal voice would attract enemy fire.

This operation was bigger than some of the others, with more than 20 SEALs on the ground. They were brought in by boat, but would likely need to be extracted by air, since the operation was quite a distance inland. Two Army Huey troop-carrying "Slicks" were on standby at the base, but their crews were housed several minutes away from the airfield.

As Ray sat in the trailer about midnight, the whispered call "Scramble 1" came in from the SEAL Team over the radio. The Fire Team Leader, LCDR Myers, took the call and hit the alarm button on the wall to alert the enlisted crew in the other trailer as Ray dashed out the door. Myers phoned the hooch where the Army Huey pilots were housed to alert them to the emergency. Ray got into the copilot's seat on the left side of the aircraft, pushed the battery switch to the "On" position and hit the starter. As the blades began to spin Myers got into the pilot's seat, buckling himself in. The other crewmen had already jumped into the back of the helicopter, ready to go. After the engine started the pilot took over the controls and Ray buckled his belt/harness. Within a few seconds they were in the air. This was a mission to extract the SEALs and not just a fire suppression mission.

Ray's assignment as copilot was to handle airborne radio communications and navigation while the two helicopters headed to the scene of the engagement. Within fifteen minutes they were approaching the SEAL team, who were in heavy combat with the enemy. Ray called the team radio operator on the F.M. radio in order to let them know they had arrived and to determine their exact location and to ask where they wanted the fire. They could see tracer fire on the ground and soon the SEALs fired a long line of tracers in the direction of where the fire suppression was needed.

The gunships came in low and fast over the area. Ray flipped down the gunsight for the M60's and opened up with the four machineguns when they were over the area. The pilot fired rockets from his cyclic control. The other gunship was doing the same as they swept the area with fire. The Army Hueys were still a few minutes away so the gunships circled and came in again, raking the area with fire. They fired close to the SEALs, within 30' of their positions. It had to be this close, because the Viet Cong were nearly on top of the men. The gunships made at least four or five runs, keeping the enemy at bay, buying time for the men on the ground until the Army Hueys arrived.

The Army did arrive, calling in their location as they approached the area. Ray talked to them on the radio, giving the exact location of the SEALs and told them where to land. There was only room for one helicopter at a time to land. As the first slick approached the LZ (landing zone) the two gunships came in behind, then raked the area on both sides with gunfire, as the slick briefly touched down and a group of SEALs jumped aboard. As the overloaded slick left the area, Ray could see the SEALs in the helicopter, still shooting at the enemy on the ground. These were some tough guys.

The gunships came around again, led by the second slick. Once again the gunships opened up with their murderous fire on both sides as the remaining SEALs jumped onto the helicopter. As the slick lumbered off Ray watched this group of SEALs firing their weapons out the door of the helicopter.

All managed to get out of the area safely. Ray later heard that about two dozen SEALs were on the ground and that about half of them were wounded, but none lost their lives. They all flew to Dong Tam, where the wounded were treated. Moose later told him the mission was considered a success.[1]

For Ray, this was just another mission. They were particularly fortunate that night, because there were no injuries to the men on the helicopters and they were able to extract all of the SEALs. He suffered a minor wound to his head and face during his tour, on February 19, 1968, when a bullet came through the cockpit, spraying his face with shrapnel. This didn't stop him from completing his 1-year tour in July 1968.

Fig 43 - Ray with minor injuries, pointing to hole in windscreen after February 19, 1968 mission.

Ray stayed in the Navy until 1977, obtaining his Bachelor of Science degree while still in the Navy. He had a variety of "careers" after that and worked for General Motors, Rockwell and McDonnell-Douglas. In 1996, he moved to the San Francisco Bay Area and eventually got a job with Pacific Bell where he was a manager for Special Projects, until his retirement in 2010. Ray is a member of American Legion Post 246, a docent for the Veterans Memorial Building in Danville, California and an active member of Viet Nam Veterans of Diablo Valley. He lives in Livermore, California. [2]

Fig 44 - Ray La Rochelle today

NOTES AND REFERENCES

[1] Ray later learned that the SEAL team came upon a force of approximately 2200 Viet Cong, a much larger force than anyone anticipated. The emergency situation occurred when a sentry fired on the team, prompting the call.

[2] Ray La Rochelle was interviewed for this story on 11/16/15. Since most of the SEAL missions were classified, the exact date of the mission is unknown.

Chapter Nine

Mig-21 Attack

Bill Kiper saw a brief glint of shiny metal through his windscreen. It was a few thousand feet below him, but it was definitely another jet, accelerating and climbing in his direction. Bill was a Navy fighter pilot, flying his F-8 Crusader. It was early February 1968 and the Vietnam War was raging. He felt the rush of adrenaline as the other plane got closer and he recognized the outline of a Mig-21, a Russian-made high performance jet that was not often seen. The Mig continued in his direction, its pilot now having seen him. It was going to be a fight.

In Bill's two carrier cruises to Vietnam he had never seen a Mig in flight, let alone the Mig-21. His first cruise was in 1964 aboard the carrier *USS Ranger*. In fact, Bill was in the air when the Gulf of Tonkin incident occurred, but that is another story. His second cruise was in 1965 on the *USS Bon Homme Richard*. On these cruises, which included many regular flights over North Vietnam and South Vietnam, the North Vietnamese weren't too interested in engaging the American fighters, especially the F-8 Crusader that Bill flew. The F-8, unlike earliest versions of its F-4 Phantom contemporary, had guns and missiles, where the Phantom had just missiles. The missiles often failed, leaving the Phantom defenseless. The North Vietnamese knew this and didn't like to engage the gun-toting Crusaders. The only Migs Bill saw were Mig-17s on the ground, at airfields, sometimes taxiing to take off. The rules of engagement, unfair as they were, didn't permit American pilots to attack the Migs until they were an airborne threat.[1]

Bill was born in Arkansas in 1934 and his mother died when he was just a month old. He was raised by an aunt and

uncle until he was 12, when his father remarried and the family moved to Spokane, Washington with his brother and sister. After graduating from high school he attended Washington State College, majoring in electrical engineering. He found electrical engineering boring, so after

FIG 45 - BILL KIPER IN FLIGHT TRAINING

college he decided to pursue a more interesting future, that of a U.S. Navy fighter pilot. He has never regretted the decision.

After flight training Bill flew the FJ3, (the Navy's version of the F-86 Sabre), which was the fastest, most advanced jet in the Navy's arsenal at the time. Two years later he received orders to report to Moffett Field, to VF 124, the fighter squadron that became the training ground for the new F-8 Crusader, capable of speeds in excess of 1,000 miles per hour. He soon found himself an instructor pilot in the F-8, initially assigned to Moffett Field and then to Miramar Naval Air Station (NAS). By this time he had met and married his wife, Karin. The two early cruises to Vietnam would follow.

FIG 46 - BILL KIPER LATER IN HIS F-8 OVER TAHOE IN VF 302

Now here he was, finally engaging a Mig. Both planes made violent turning maneuvers, trying to get the upper hand. What followed was a series of high G twists, turns, climbs and dives. Bill used every maneuver in his training manual to gain the advantage. It was exhausting. His opponent was very skilled, reacting and counteracting every movement that Bill made, using the Mig's advantage to turn tightly. This went on for several minutes, but the Mig was finally able to slip in behind him. Bill knew it was over for him, even before he heard the announcement "Op away" on the radio, which signaled the Mig had locked him into its sight.

This engagement didn't occur over the skies of North Vietnam, but high over the Nevada desert! The announcement ending the engagement was by fellow Navy pilot Tom Cassidy, Bill's friend who was flying the Mig. It was a secret testing program called "Have Doughnut". The location where the engagement took place was about 85 miles north of Las Vegas, near an airfield called Groom Lake. The public now knows this place as Area 51.[2]

Where this Mig came from is a story in itself. In 1966 an Iraqi fighter pilot, Munir Redfa, defected, flying his Mig-21 to Israel. The Israeli Air Force evaluated the aircraft and then loaned it to the U.S. government. Our government took the plane to Nevada for secret testing and evaluation. It was secret because we didn't want the Soviets to know we had acquired the aircraft, even temporarily.[3]

For Bill it all started when he received a phone call at Miramar concerning a secret project. He was asked to select another flight instructor and to report to Nellis Air Force Base in Nevada, with two F-8 Crusader jets. The mission, and the details were sketchy, but he was asked to give his commanding officer only the most basic information. He agreed, but wondered what his boss would say. He needn't have worried because his commanding officer had also received a call.

Bill chose Jerry Unruh, an excellent instructor pilot, as his wingman and flew to Nellis Air Force Base in early February of 1968. He arrived to find that other Navy and Air Force pilots had received the same request, bringing their planes with them. All the pilots would be engaging in mock combat with the latest, most advanced fighter in the Communist arsenal, the Mig-21 "Fishbed". Among those included for testing were the F-4 Phantom, the F-105 Thunderchief, the F-111 Aardvark, the F-100 Super Saber, the F-104 Starfighter, the F-5A Freedom Fighter, RF-101 Voodoo, RF-4C Phantom, B-66 Destroyer, the F-8 Crusader, A-4 Skyhawk, A-6 Intruder and A-7 Corsair.[4]

There weren't just pilots involved in this testing, but many other experts as well, primarily engineers and other technical people. In addition, high ranking military officers were there, including Navy admirals and Air Force generals. There was a lengthy debriefing after every flight, which often lasted hours.

The U.S. aircraft and personnel were based at Nellis Air Force Base, while the Mig -21 was housed at Groom Lake. After Bill's first dogfight ended in defeat, the planes separated and came toward each other again, passing nose-to-nose. This signaled the beginning of another dogfight. This continued until both planes were low on fuel, at which time both aircraft returned to base. After the first encounter, Mig pilot Tom Cassidy sent Bill a photo from the Mig gun camera, with Bill's F-8 centered in the gunsight. Cassidy captioned it with "Check your '6' Bill", which meant that Bill should check his 6 o'clock position or look behind him. It was a humiliating moment for him, but he took it good-naturedly. (See photo)

The first few flights ended in the same fashion. Bill was following the rules, using the same principles that were taught to students in training. He lost every early engagement. This happened with other pilots in other aircraft as well. They needed to learn new tactics. At this point, with the input of everyone involved, new section tactics involving two planes were developed that allowed one fighter to gain an advantage over the Mig for a successful kill. These tactics worked well during the final engagements.[5]

At the end of February, Bill and Jerry Unruh returned to Miramar, armed with new knowledge and tactics.

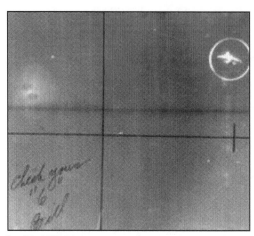

FIG 47 - MIG-21 GUN CAMERA PHOTO

Meanwhile, a film was being made about lessons learned over the Nevada desert. A few weeks later, with this training film in hand, Bill and a Navy F-4 pilot, Sam Leeds, who had also participated in the exercise in Nevada, were sent to the Tonkin Gulf to inform fighter pilots on two carriers what they learned about engaging the Mig-21.

One of the main things that Bill and Jerry Unruh took away from the experience and passed on to the other pilots was a key component to success in engaging the Mig-21. This was the concept of "energy maneuverability", which translated into the need for either altitude or airspeed, preferably both. Soon the Mig-21 began appearing more frequently in the skies over North Vietnam and the pilots were better prepared to engage them, now armed with new tactics and more knowledge of the Mig's flight characteristics.

One of the outcomes of "Have Doughnut" was that the Navy realized its shortcomings in training fighter pilots. A year after the testing in Nevada the U.S. Navy Fighter

Weapons School, more commonly known as "Top Gun" was formed at Miramar Naval Air Station. Its purpose was to teach advanced fighter weapons tactics, those same tactics that were learned in the Nevada skies.

Before Bill's second cruise in the Tonkin Gulf had ended, Bill was notified that his wife was very ill, following the birth of their son. He was directed to return to San Diego immediately and 26 hours later he was at the hospital in San Diego with his wife. It was at that point that he was reassigned to Air Wing 12, as an instructor in the F-8 and F-4 fighters. This was how he came to be at Miramar when he received the call to report to Nellis.

FIG 48 - BILL KIPER LATER IN HIS CAREER

Bill realized it would be quite a while before he could make any long, ship-board cruises. As the result of his family situation he decided to leave active duty. A year later he was released from active duty and was subsequently hired as a pilot by United Airlines.

During this same general time period, from 1969-1973, he served as a consultant at the Naval Weapons Center, China Lakes. In addition, he joined the Naval Air Reserve at N.A.S. Los Alamitos, California, where he flew the F-4 Phantom.

A short time later that unit was disbanded because the aircraft were needed to replace combat losses in Vietnam. He then joined the newly formed Reserve unit at Miramar. In short order he was selected to form a new F-8 Reserve unit there, VF 302 and to serve as its commander.

It would be a squadron that would stay ready for combat. He was allowed to choose Navy pilots who had been on active duty and who were leaving or had left the Navy. Each one had served at least two combat tours in Vietnam. Bill stayed in the Naval Reserve, retiring as a captain after 21 years of service.[6]

Today Bill is also retired from United Airlines. He and Karin have a son, a daughter and four grandchildren. They live in Alamo, California. In addition to being a member of the Vietnam Veterans of Diablo Valley, Bill is a member of the Tailhook Association and the Alamo, California Rotary.

FIG 49 - BILL KIPER TODAY WITH F-8 ON THE USS HORNET

NOTES AND REFERENCES

[1] Some later versions of the F-4 were equipped with external gun pods and finally, an internal cannon.

[2] The Navy also referred to the location as "Site A".

[3] Much of the background from the "Have Doughnut" project, including how the Mig was obtained, came from R.D. Thornton's book, *Migs Over Nevada*. Bill was given a different cover story on how the Mig was obtained.

[4] Bill's primary role was engaging the Mig-21 with his F-8 Crusader, but his flight

log shows he also flew the F-4 for two engagements, on 2/24/68 and 2/25/68.

[5] In addition to studying dogfighting characteristics and tactics, the Mig-21's overall performance was evaluated along with things such as its cannon performance against ground targets. Bill Kiper's role was that of flying the F-8 and developing new tactics to combat the Mig in the air.

[6] Bill Kiper was interviewed for this story in Alamo, California on 2/29/16 and 3/4/16, with a follow-up phone interview on 3/7/16.

Chapter Ten

I Didn't Even Know His Name

FIG 50 - PRIVATE BILL LAVIGNE

Bill LaVigne was born in Seattle, Washington, and spent his early years in the Northwest with his parents and three younger siblings. His father was a WWII Vet and D-Day survivor with a restless spirit and they moved around a lot. Bill attended 13 different elementary schools by the time he was in 5th grade. Then they moved to Redding, California, where his father settled down somewhat. Bill attended high school in Redding. He knew he would be drafted so he volunteered for the draft and was inducted on February 1, 1967. He was trained as an infantryman. It was just a few months before he found himself in Vietnam, arriving on the 4th of July. He was assigned to a unit known as "Quarter Cav". Bill LaVigne was in "B" Troop, 1st

Squadron, 4th Cavalry Regiment, 1st Infantry Division. Unlike their predecessors they did not ride horses, but went to war and fought the enemy in tanks and "tracks" (tracked Armored Personnel Carriers or APCs). Bill was a little bit like a fish out of water in the unit. Most of the others had armor specialties or MOS. He was an infantryman that just happened to get assigned to the unit when he arrived in Vietnam.

FIG 51 - TANK FROM B TROOP WITH BATTLE DAMAGE

There were three tanks and seven tracks in B Troop. The tanks were M48 Patton tanks and the official name for the tracks was M113 personnel carrier. Nobody seemed to want to drive the tracks so Bill volunteered to be the driver of one of the tracks.

Each vehicle had a 4-man crew. Bill was the only one who was actually inside the vehicle. The other three men rode on top. One of the soldiers, the TC or tank commander, manned the .50 caliber machinegun, one manned an M60 machinegun and one normally carried an M-79 grenade launcher. If he didn't carry the grenade launcher he carried an M-16 rifle.

The tracks could also carry infantrymen into battle, but his troop rarely did. They served as a rapid response unit in some cases. The infantry went out on patrols, trying to flush out and engage the enemy and B troop was called into the fight with their firepower to destroy the enemy. When the vehicle was in a stationary position in battle Bill's assignment was taking care of the ammo for the .50 caliber gun, connecting the belts of ammo and changing the barrel for the gunner if the gun overheated. When they weren't in battle, he also was in charge of the beer cooler. He much preferred that assignment, even though there was no ice available.

They named their track "Brenda". After his arrival in Vietnam he was in combat most of the time. Their area of operations was the Iron Triangle, north of Saigon, which was heavily infested with the enemy. Highway 13, also known as Thunder Road, ran through their area of operations. They provided security for convoys traveling through, ran search and destroy missions on their own and responded to the needs of the infantry when they came under attack. It kept them very busy most of the time and they rarely got a break. He recalls that he didn't get a hot shower or have an opportunity to get really clean for three months, but body odor and cleanliness were the least of his worries. Staying alive was much more important.

Fig 52 - "Brenda", Bill's M113 armored personnel carrier

By early 1968, Bill was a seasoned combat soldier. B troop had been lucky as far as casualties were concerned, although several had been wounded. Some had finished their tours and rotated home and replacements filled their positions. In mid-April they were set up at a camp in the Iron Triangle. They had staged out of this area for about a week and were getting hit regularly by rockets and sniper fire from somewhere in the jungle outside their perimeter. It was annoying, to say the least, but so far there hadn't been any casualties that Bill was aware of.

There were several new guys who had recently arrived. One of the new guys, who was very friendly and likable, started following Bill around. He was interested in learning as much as possible and he was like Bill's shadow and stuck to him "like glue" in Bill's words. He later reflected that this trooper chose him because he was one of the senior guys who had a lot of experience and knew how to stay alive.

One night a man was chosen from each track in B Troop to go out on a night time ambush patrol mission. Bill was the lucky guy chosen from his track and he saw that his "shadow"

FIG 53 - BILL LAVIGNE WITH CAPTURED AK-47

was also chosen for the mission. The 10 men met with a Green Beret captain to be briefed. The briefing was very detailed and thorough and, as Bill listened intently, he thought to himself that this guy really knew his stuff and was well-prepared to lead the mission. He felt very comfortable going out on the patrol with the captain, this professional soldier, even though he didn't know him. After several minutes the briefing neared its end. The captain walked over to Bill, patted him on the shoulder, said "I'm sure you'll do fine", and walked away. Bill was shocked! He had assumed the captain would lead the patrol, not him. Sure, he was an infantryman and had been on numerous ambush patrols, but hadn't led these patrols. He was a Specialist 4th Class and there were nine NCO's (sergeants) above him in the unit who could lead the patrol, so why him? He didn't understand, but he got the men ready and prepared to leave.

Seven of the men were recent arrivals, including his "shadow". Bill was going to carry the M60 machinegun and chose the "shadow" as his ammo bearer so he could be nearby. One of the experienced men would be the first or point man, followed by Bill, with the ammo bearer directly behind him. The others, mostly newer replacement troops, would follow.

After dark, when it was time to leave they left through the gate, single file. Concertina wire formed the perimeter of the makeshift base. They walked for several yards before making a right turn, and started walking parallel to the perimeter. They hadn't walked far when one of the men stepped on a trip wire, setting off a stationary flare, which lit up the entire area.

Immediately, from within the camp an M60 machinegun and a .50 caliber machinegun opened up on them. All 10 men hit the ground, hugging the ground as closely as possible, as yells broke out from inside the perimeter to stop firing. The M60 stopped, but the .50 caliber fired for several more seconds, then stopped.

Bill waited for several seconds until the firing stopped, then slowly and carefully picked himself up, trying to make sense of what had just happened. He looked around and saw that the other men were also getting up, that is, all except one. Shadow lay motionless in the dirt, face down, right alongside him. Bill knelt down and turned him over. Beneath Shadow's right eye was a bullet wound. He had been struck by a ricochet. Bill yelled, "Doc" and the medic, who was one of the men on patrol with him, came over. Doc checked Shadow's vital signs, looked up at Bill and said,, "He's dead."

This couldn't be. Just a few minutes earlier he was alive, following closely behind Bill. If he had been in a different position, maybe he'd be alive. But he was so close because Bill had chosen him to be his ammo bearer, and now he was dead. They were all stunned, all in shock.

One of the men produced a poncho and laid it on the ground. They picked Shadow up and carefully laid him on the poncho. Bill grabbed one corner of the poncho and three others picked up the other corners and slowly and quietly carried the limp, lifeless body toward the concertina wire perimeter of the camp. Others walked ahead and stomped on the concertina wire, pressing it down so the men could walk over it. The men inside the wire quietly watched through the darkness. Bill, still in shock from what had happened, recalls thinking, "I knew that God spared my life." In his mind this was the only possible reason for his survival.

The men walked for a distance inside the wire and slowly and gently placed the poncho on the ground. As the men stood quietly around the poncho, a soldier from A Troop, the troop responsible for guarding that section of the perimeter, ran up. He was sobbing. Out of the sobs came the words, "I'm sorry. I'm so sorry". One of the B troopers from the patrol smacked the A trooper in the head, knocking him to the ground.

It was so wrong! Everything about this was so wrong. The A trooper wasn't involved in this. He hadn't fired the shots. Those firing the shots didn't want to kill a fellow American. It was simply a tragic mistake and nothing could change it.

A few minutes later the colonel came up. He tried to give the nine survivors, still in shock, a pep talk. The Green Beret captain, their own lieutenant and a senior sergeant accompanied him and stood by while the colonel talked. What is certain is that none of them were in the mood for a pep talk. It was the last thing they needed or wanted. Then it dawned on Bill as the colonel continued to speak. He wanted them to go out on patrol again! They had just lost one of their own because of a tragic mistake and he expected them to go out and finish the patrol. Insane!

Bill exploded. He recalls the exact words he said but they can't be repeated. The words and his tone were definitely insubordinate. Among other things he told them there were others, including the colonel, who could go out on patrol. Finally, the officers and the sergeant just walked away. He and the others didn't go out that night and no formal action was taken for his outburst, but for the next 10 or 11 nights in a row Bill was assigned to duties outside the wire. He heard later that the man from A troop who manned the .50 caliber machinegun and fired that fateful and fatal shot that killed Shadow had a mental breakdown shortly after the incident and was sent home.

Bill finished his tour and returned to the U.S. on July 4, 1968. He realized this "friendly fire" incident had defined his life, so to speak. When he came home he was stationed at Fort Carson, Colorado. He was there for a few months and was restless, like many returning combat Vets. He received an early hardship discharge from the Army on November 1st of that year, three months ahead of his scheduled discharge date, after 21 months of service because his father was very ill and unable to care for the family.

Bill's father was a commercial fisherman and Bill took over his father's boat, working in the fishing industry in Oregon for the next 20 years. Finally, the boat sank and he went to work for a national moving company, eventually becoming an independent mover, which he is doing today in northern California. Bill is divorced and has four sons. He lives in Vallejo, California and is active in the Viet Nam Veterans of Diablo Valley.

Rarely a day goes by without Bill thinking of that young man who died that night in Vietnam. There were others lost, but this one always sticks out in his mind because it was particularly tragic. He doesn't remember the man's name and likely didn't know it then. Over the past 48 years he has tried to identify the trooper, with requests through the V.A., examining unit records and even talking to men who served with him. The memory is even more difficult because he can't even put a name with his memory.[1]

(Author's note: During the making of this story the author was able to locate records confirming the specific date of the incident (April 19, 1968) and identified the soldier as PFC Charles C. Beard. Bill is now trying to locate the family and hopes to eventually meet with them.)[2]

FIG 54 - BILL LAVIGNE TODAY

NOTES AND REFERENCES

[1] The author interviewed Bill LaVigne for this story on 11/7/16

[2] The search was more difficult because of the nature of the soldier's death (friendly fire) and the fact that his name was not in some of the records. Beard's official date of death is listed as 4/19/68, so it's the same incident referenced in the 4th Cav log for the evening of 4/19/68. The Vietnam Virtual Wall website lists Beards death on that same date was a result of "Misadventure (Friendly Fire)." The Operations log for Quarter Cav lists a patrol from B Troop leaving the perimeter at 1930 hours and at 2000 hours it indicates that one man was "seriously hurt, coming back". The next entry said "Died before getting to the wire. Investigation started." No name was listed and no details were given regarding how the injury occurred, adding to the confusion, making it difficult to identify the soldier.

Chapter Eleven

A Decent Proposal

It was one of those love stories you hear about from time to time. Bill Green fell in love with Peggy when she was still in high school in San Francisco. He first met her in January 1966, through a friend, at a neighborhood gathering. She was a junior and he graduated from high school the previous year. For Bill it was love at first sight. Peggy's first impression wasn't as strong. Peggy describes her initial feelings as "curious and mildly interested." They began dating shortly thereafter.

Bill wanted to go into the military and tried to enlist in the Army, but didn't pass the physical in early 1967. He received his draft notice just a few months later and was drafted into the U.S. Army in August. The standards for being drafted, as the Vietnam War was heating up, were less stringent than for enlistments. A few short months later he finished training and knew he was bound for Vietnam. He knew he wanted to marry Peggy, but also knew he didn't want to leave a young widow should anything happen to him. He proposed and she accepted, with a plan that they would get married when he returned from Vietnam..

FIG 55 - BILL GREEN IN VIETNAM

So Bill went off to war in January 1968, barely a month after he proposed. He was soon in the thick of it, an infantryman in the 198th Light Infantry Brigade, part of the 23rd Infantry Division. His mission was simple, to search out and destroy the enemy. He was stationed in the far north of South Vietnam. His home was the jungle. He became good at his mission, better than his enemy who had that same mission. The proof was in survival.

He was rarely at a base camp, but spent most of his time in the field, on one occasion staying out for 31 days. Bill felt comfortable with his instincts and was chosen to be the point man, the guy in front on the patrol, the first one to see and engage the enemy, the first one to encounter booby traps, mines and whatever lay ahead. He preferred being up front. He was confident in his abilities. By being up front he was more in control of his own destiny, and that of the others in his squad. Contact with the enemy was regular and often intense. Within a few months he was promoted to sergeant.

He wrote to Peggy regularly. Most of the letters were written from the jungle. He didn't tell her much about the war, but told her how much he loved her…and how much he missed her. Peggy also wrote to Bill regularly. She noticed that the tone in his letters gradually changed. No longer was he the fun-loving boyfriend with the comical stories that had gone off to war. He was more serious. Gone was the sense of humor that she loved, but she still loved him...and she worried, especially after one letter.

Peggy watched the TV coverage of the war with her dad. The news media covered the war every single day, often showing footage of the actual ongoing battles. They also focused on the losses. There was major coverage of the Tet Offensive, which began at the end of January and continued through February of 1968. This was the largest battle to date in Vietnam. The news media had begun to turn against the war now, which became obvious from the way the stories were covered. Peggy's dad liked Bill. One of the things he told her was that even if her feelings changed, she was not to break up with Bill while he was at war. There would be no "Dear John" letters sent from his home. She had no intention of breaking up with Bill, but she did worry, more so after seeing the battles raging on television. Bill didn't refer to the war much in his letters, but in May 1968 he wrote a letter where he referenced a tough battle he had been in at a place called Kham Duc. He didn't mention things like this very often so she knew it must have been a *bad* situation.

A few nights after she received the letter she went out to a night club with her sister. In the club was a young soldier in uniform, not a very common sight in San Francisco. She overheard him talking about just getting home from Vietnam.

She and her sister approached him and bought him a drink. He started talking to the girls and told them his job was cleaning up after battles. He said the worst was a place called Kham Duc. The soldier said that no one survived the battle, that all the Americans were killed.

Peggy told him she was happy to get a letter from her boyfriend a few days ago who was at Kham Duc and learned that he made it out alive. The soldier replied that he was there and said "I can tell you that no one made it out alive." Although she knew that Bill had

Fig 56 - Bill Green taking a break in Vietnam

survived she was more worried than ever when she went home that night.[1]

The truth was that it had been a fierce battle, etched in his mind enough that Bill dropped his guard and mentioned it when he wrote to her. He and his company were brought in to Kham Duc by Chinook helicopters. They were engaged in three days of intense fighting there. He didn't want her to worry and had no way of knowing that she'd run into some soldier that wasn't there for the fighting, but who had come in after the fighting was over and for some reason felt a need to embellish the story. The battle needed no embellishments.

Bill missed Peggy so much and wanted more than anything to marry her. He wanted something to hold on to and didn't want to wait. The longer he was away, the more intense were his feelings. He couldn't predict what would happen in the future. He had already been wounded once, but the wound was minor and he was sent back into combat. So in another letter written from the jungle Bill asked Peggy what she thought about getting married. If she accepted he'd apply for a leave to go to Hawaii and they could get married there. Even though he would have to return to Vietnam, he would have something to look forward to on his return, something to keep him going, a reason to survive. In a follow-up letter she did accept his proposal.[2]

Mostly it was the married guys in Bill's unit who were granted leave in Hawaii, but Bill applied and was happy when his request was accepted. He'd be going on R&R to Honolulu, Hawaii, in September. He provided the date to Peggy in another letter so she could make plans and flight reservations. They were both Catholic, so Peggy went to her church to get permission from the priest to marry Bill. Much to her chagrin, the priest refused to give his approval. She returned home broken-hearted. They were both in good standing with the church and wanted it to be a sacramental marriage, with the blessings of the church. She didn't know what to do. Her father had the answer, telling her there was more than one priest in the Catholic Church. She went to another church and the priest readily gave his approval.

One of the church requirements was for both of them to complete a marriage preparation class. Peggy enrolled to complete the class. There were no marriage preparation classes being given in the jungles of Vietnam, but Bill spoke to his chaplain on one of his few days back at base camp and the chaplain waived this requirement for him. So for Bill it was now just a matter of waiting...and staying alive.

Two days before his departure date Bill left his squad and was sent back to Headquarters Company. He was driven to Chu Lai. His uniform had been prepared for him, a nice clean uniform complete with ribbons. From Chu Lai he flew by helicopter to Da Nang, to the R&R Center there. While waiting for the flight that would take him to Hawaii, he started playing poker with some of the other men. He won several hundred dollars and also won some civilian clothes. Both would be helpful on his honeymoon. Finally the plane arrived to take him to Hawaii. It was a TWA Boeing 707. He and the other lucky soldiers boarded the plane that would take them from a war zone and hours later deposit them in a peaceful, tropical paradise.

Meanwhile, Peggy boarded her flight in San Francisco. Here she was, all of 19 years of age, flying by herself to Hawaii, full of youth and hope, yet understanding that Bill was different than when he left home. She had noted some changes in the tone of his letters. Were there other changes? Just how much had he changed? She wanted to marry the man she knew, but was this the man she knew, or was it someone else? Was this the right thing to do or was she making a mistake? All of these thoughts crossed her mind as she in sat her seat, looking out the window at the vast expanse of Pacific Ocean.

The mood on Bill's plane was boisterous and happy. They were headed back to the world, back to civilization, away from the stinking jungles of Vietnam. Bill was more quiet than most of the others on the plane. He was really happy to be seeing Peggy again, to realize his dream of marrying her, something he thought of every day, but all of this was so confusing.

Peggy arrived the day before Bill. She anxiously awaited his arrival at the airport terminal, still very nervous about their first meeting after all these months. Unlike civilian flights, where the passengers simply went into the terminal to meet loved ones, when the soldiers came off the plane, they were initially taken into a holding room for a short briefing about the do's and don'ts while they were in Hawaii. The sergeant who gave the briefing talked to the men about acceptable behavior, the date and time they had to be back for the return trip to Vietnam and various logistical issues.

Meanwhile, Peggy waited and waited. The soldiers began streaming out that door, happy, with loved ones waiting for some of them. There must have been 200 or more. She watched as each one came through the door, watching for Bill. Slowly the number of men coming out dwindled. A few stragglers came out, but Bill wasn't among them. What was wrong? Didn't he make the flight? Had he been wounded or worse yet, had he been killed in those last few days when she hadn't heard from him?

Finally a sergeant came through the door, obviously someone in charge. She hurried up to him, telling him her fiancé was supposed to be on the plane, but he wasn't there. What had happened?! The sergeant said he thought everyone had already left, but he'd check and went back into the large room, closing the door.

Bill had gotten off the plane with the other men, trying to make sense of what was happening. Just two days earlier he was engaged in combat in a tropical jungle, with all the associated dangers of ambushes, punji stakes, booby traps, and also the smells. Here he was now, in a crisp, clean uniform, walking into an air-conditioned building, where there was no danger, no one waiting around the corner to shoot at him. It was just too much to digest. As much as he wanted to see Peggy, as much as he wanted to marry Peggy, he just couldn't go through that door, not yet. He sat down, unsure of what to do, uneasy, trying to make sense of it all and lost in thought. Here he was, the place he dreamed of being, back "in the world", but in his head he was still in Vietnam. He had to sort this out before going through the door.

Several minutes later, as he sat there alone, an older, senior sergeant came back into the room, the same man who had briefed them on the rules earlier. The sergeant sat down next to him, waiting a moment before speaking and then said, "Sergeant, there's a young lady waiting for you out there. Get outta here. Go enjoy yourself." With that encouragement, but still a little apprehensive, Bill stood up and walked through the door.

They embraced, excited to be together again. He felt much better now, holding beehive-haired Peggy. They didn't have a lot of time, though. Peggy wasn't thrilled with Bill's handlebar mustache, so she asked him to cut it off before they got married. Bill wasn't thrilled with Peggy's hairdo, so one of their first compromises in their long relationship was when Peggy changed her hairdo and Bill cut off his mustache. They quickly obtained their marriage license. After doing so they went to Fort DeRussy, where an Army chaplain married them. The date was September 19, 1968. Bill felt like he was on "Cloud 9". He was able to relax for those two days that followed. They truly enjoyed their brief honeymoon. They went sightseeing at Waikiki and just enjoyed their time together, even though this place called Vietnam was looming in the background.

Peggy didn't doubt that she made the right decision. Sure, there were some changes, but he was still the man she loved.

Fig 57 - Bill and Peggy Green wedding photo (Sept 1968)

Those three days passed too quickly and it was soon time for Bill to return to the airport for the long flight back to Vietnam. Bill described it as a feeling of emptiness when he left her. All too soon he was back in the war.

On Bill's return he was taken out of combat. He wasn't happy about this. He wanted to be in the field with his buddies. They worked well together. They were a team and took care of each other. Instead, Bill was now back at the fire base, handling radio traffic and supervising other soldiers who handled the radio traffic. It was frustrating not to be with his men, especially during the calls for help, but it was also safer. Peggy was happy about that.

When Bill's year-long tour was nearly up, he still had slightly more than 6 months left on his 2-year commitment in the Army. At that time the Army was letting men out on their return to the U.S. when they had less than 6 months left to serve. Bill was offered, and considered, the option of staying in Vietnam just one more month, so he'd be discharged as soon as he returned home. Peggy wanted nothing of it; she wanted him home and safe. So he returned home in January 1969 and finally got out of the Army in August 1969.

Bill became an electrician and worked in that trade until his retirement in 2002. Bill and Peggy have two children and two grandchildren. They live in Alamo, California. Bill is involved in many Veteran projects. One of the most noteworthy is being a volunteer mentor for returning combat Vets at the Concord, California Vets Center. He is also a co-director of the Speakers Bureau for the Viet Nam Veterans of Diablo Valley. Bill eventually won the battle over the mustache and sports one today, but Peggy never reprised the beehive hairdo.[3]

Fig 58 - Bill and Peggy Green today

NOTES AND REFERENCES

[1] Kham Duc was a Special Forces camp near the Laotian border. The battle took place May 10-12, 1968. The camp was in danger of being overrun and Bill's unit was called in to assist.

[2] He was wounded a second time, but again the wound was minor and didn't keep him out of combat.

[3] Bill and Peggy Green were interviewed for this story on 11/19/15.

Chapter Twelve

Pleiku, A Far Cry from Bozeman

It happened many years ago. She was a little apprehensive that night when she walked to the front of the room. Allison Howells didn't usually speak to groups of men like this. There were a few women in the room, but not many. She looked around the room as she stood by the podium, wondering what they were thinking. As she was being introduced, an incredible thing happened. Before she had a chance to say anything, before she could even greet the group, everyone in the room stood and began clapping. The realization set in...they were clapping for her. This group was honoring her for her service in a combat zone in Vietnam. It still moves her today when she thinks about it. [1]

Allison was an Army nurse. She was born in Bozeman, Montana, and grew up there. When she finished high school she attended Montana State College, also in Bozeman, graduating in 1967 with a degree in nursing. Even then she had a plan, which had three different goals. Part one was just getting out of Bozeman. Her entire life had been spent in and around Bozeman. Part two was getting practical nursing experience. Even when she was a nursing student she knew she wanted to work in public health, but to get there she needed hospital experience. Part three was that she wanted to see the world, she wanted to go to places she had never seen, meet people she'd never met.

She realized the Army could help her accomplish these goals, so she enlisted in the U.S. Army Nursing Corps when she finished college, a 3-year enlistment. After training, while stationed in Fort Gordon, Georgia, she volunteered to go to Europe, realizing she may not get her choice of assignments. She didn't. In September 1968 the 24 year-old nurse arrived in Vietnam. Once there she did have her choice of hospitals and chose the 71st Evacuation Hospital in Pleiku.

FIG 59 - LT. ALLISON HOWELLS

This hospital was really a huge trauma center, set up to handle the mass casualties that were occurring in the skirmishes and larger battles in the Central Highlands of South Vietnam. When she arrived in this foreign land, her first impression was of the poverty in and around Pleiku. There wasn't much time for first impressions, though, because there was a war on and American soldiers to care for. Soon she was immersed with the task of saving soldiers' lives. Other impressions of Vietnam and the war would follow.

Soon after her arrival she began treating the wounded, who arrived by helicopter. Everyone could hear the helicopters approaching so there was no real need for any other sort of announcement. All available staff ran to the helipads as the helicopters arrived to unload their precious and damaged human cargo. Triage was critical for the handling of these men, prioritizing the care for these young soldiers. There were three major categories, those with the most severe wounds demanding immediate emergency treatment, those less seriously wounded, and those for whom no treatment could help. This third category was the most difficult and one of her recurring memories is of a young soldier who fell into this category.

He was an enlisted man in his mid-20's. He had been horribly burned in a helicopter crash. She didn't know how it occurred and didn't know any of the details, only the extent of the injuries and that he was spending his final hours with her. Allison didn't know his name, or at least wouldn't remember it after all these years. She could tell from his accent that he was from somewhere in the South and he didn't know he was dying. They gave him pain-killers, but he was still in excruciating pain, and conscious. There was nothing more anyone could do for him and that didn't make it any easier. Through his pain he talked of his love for wife and children at home, and how he was going home to them. He went home, but not alive. There were many like him, but there were also many others who survived because of the quick, excellent medical care received at Pleiku.

Allison didn't know the names of the men. The most seriously wounded were there only long enough to get them stabilized and then they were moved to a safer, longer term hospital setting. Stabilization involved many things, but often included amputation and life-saving surgeries. Once stabilized, they were often flown out and put on a hospital ship, and from there they were transferred to a hospital in Japan. She didn't keep in touch with any of them. Most were not there long enough to get to know them.

FIG 60 - ALLISON WITH A MEDEVAC HUEY

This is what she and the other nurses did, 12 hours a day, six days a week. Their days didn't end at 12 hours if casualties were coming in and extra staffing was needed. They stayed until the wounded were taken care of. That was their job. The airbase at Pleiku was a favorite target for the enemy, with its helicopters and airplanes. It wasn't an unusual occurrence for the base to be shelled while Allison was there, and there were several times she found herself under her bed, wearing a flak jacket and waiting for the rocket attack to stop. It's just the way it was in a combat zone. The hospital wasn't hit while she was there, at least she wasn't aware of any hits.

It wasn't always busy, so there were also some more light-hearted times, even fun times. They even had a swimming pool at the base which got plenty of use. For an outing, on days off and under heavy guard, she and other medical staff would venture into nearby villages to treat local villagers with illnesses and give inoculations to children. They were always under heavy guard when they left the base.

While in Vietnam she was promoted to captain and with the promotion came the assignment of head nurse on one of the wards. The wounded with the serious wounds, those who wouldn't return to combat, were evacuated from the wards. There were also wards for those who came in sick or with relatively minor wounds, those who would recover and return to their unit.

After 14 months it was her turn to leave Vietnam. In November 1969 Captain Allison Howells arrived home, landing at Travis Air Force Base in California. The first thing she did when she got off the airplane was to find a restroom, take off her uniform and don civilian attire. These weren't good times for the military and she didn't want any problems resulting from her service. She went home on leave for two months and returned to the Bay Area for assignment. She had no illusions about staying in the Army and got out at the end of her enlistment.

A job as a public health nurse opened up and she took the job in Alameda County. She ultimately worked in case management at several hospitals in the San Francisco Bay Area, retiring from the John Muir Hospital facility in Concord several years ago.

Allison lives in Walnut Creek and has two children and four grandchildren. She volunteers her time with the Assistance League of Diablo Valley, which provides all types of assistance to local families and also participates in The Rossmoor Scholarship Foundation, which provides college scholarships to local students. She is a member of Viet Nam

Veterans of Diablo Valley and, when not spending time with family and her volunteer organizations she, plays bocce ball, bridge and likes to golf.

FIG 61 - ALLISON HOWELLS TODAY

Most of those war memories from 1968 are in the distant past, but there are still those reminders. The distinct sound of a helicopter is one of those reminders, with the "whop" of the blades. This sound still causes her to stop whatever she's doing and, for a just a brief split second, to consider running to that far off helipad to treat an American soldier. [2]

NOTES AND REFERENCES

[1] The event referenced was the February 2000 meeting of the Viet Nam Veterans of Diablo Valley.

[2] Allison Howells was interviewed for this story on 10/13/15

Chapter Thirteen

Recon Team 6 is Missing

By its name one would think that a unit with the name Detachment B-52 would be associated with the Air Force B-52 bombers that were bombing the Ho Chi Minh Trail and North Vietnam, but the unit had nothing to do with the bombers directly. It was an elite Army Special Forces group, more commonly known as Green Berets. They performed primarily a reconnaissance and counterintelligence role in South Vietnam, occasionally venturing into neighboring countries on secret missions.

Most of the men preferred not to draw attention to their unit, preferring to be known as "the quiet professionals". When one of their own, Staff Sgt. Barry Sadler, co-wrote and sang the song *Ballad of the Green Berets*, it rose to #1 on the Billboard Hot 100 song chart, and stayed there for five weeks in March and April 1966. The song was followed up by the movie *Green Berets*, released in 1968, starring John Wayne. With these two major events generating a lot of publicity, it became increasingly difficult for the Army Special Forces to maintain their low profile as "the quiet professionals". Now virtually everyone in the U.S. was familiar with the term. The Viet Cong and the North Vietnamese Army knew them as well and had some very personal encounters with them.

Detachment B-52 was a small unit within the 5th Special Forces Group. They never numbered more than 100 men and by 1969 the entire unit had only 50-60 men. Their base camp was at Nha Trang, along the southeastern coast of Vietnam, but the men were rarely there. Their missions could take them all over South Vietnam. Their operations were conducted out of Forward Operating Bases (FOBs), closer to where the actual event was taking place. It was a small, closely knit unit. If they didn't know each other personally, they at least recognized each other on sight.

In this unit, the non-commissioned officers ran most of the operations on the ground, at least the smaller ones. They operated with various groups of indigenous people in South Vietnam, with a variety of personnel, depending on the mission at hand. The typical reconnaissance patrol consisted of three Green Beret noncoms and three South Vietnamese Rangers. There were also larger operations in which two Green Berets worked with a company of South Vietnamese Rangers.[1]

There were other groups that were part of their operations. They used Nungs, a group of ethnic Chinese, whom they paid for their services. The Nungs had a reputation as good fighters and were loyal to the Special Forces men. They also used "roadrunner teams". These men were Montagnards, tribal mountain people from the Central Highlands. They dressed in North Vietnamese uniforms and were inserted by helicopter into areas to assess the strength of enemy forces. These men operated independently, without Green Berets with them and their tasks were dangerous, for obvious reasons.

Another force that was commonly used was a bomb damage assessment (BDA) force. These men were used to check out areas after a bombing or other major action to assess the damage done. There were usually a South Vietnamese Ranger Company and 2 or 3 Green Berets in this group.

Another part of the team that lived, slept and ate with the Green Berets was the Air Force Forward Air Controllers or FACs. These men were nearly always in the air above, in their small aircraft, when the Green Berets were on the ground. Their lives often depended on the FACs' ability to call in close air support when they were in contact with enemy forces. The Green Berets operated far outside of areas where artillery or naval gun support was available. There was no really safe place in Vietnam and they always operated in what was clearly hostile territory. The FACs could call upon the Navy, Air Force and Marines for the air support. For insertions and extractions, they relied upon various Army helicopter units.

Dave Richardson was one of the Green Berets assigned to Detachment B-52. He didn't enlist in the Army to join the Special Forces. He was born in Walters, Oklahoma, spent several years on a farm in Arkansas, moved back to Oklahoma for a few years and eventually moved with his family to Mulvane, Kansas. He had two sisters and he graduated from Mulvane High School in 1967.

The draft was in full swing when Dave graduated and he decided to enlist in the Army several weeks later, on July 6, 1967. After attending his basic training he attended advanced schooling to become a radio operator. He received orders to go to Germany, but was given the option of going to jump school (parachute training) if he wanted to delay going overseas. He elected to go to jump school. As he neared completion of this training, the writing was on the wall that it

 was likely the men would be sent to Vietnam when they finished.

One day he was on a long and exhausting physical training run of several miles. The instructor was waiting for the men and told the group that anyone not wanting to run back to base should talk to "this man". This man turned out to be with Special Forces and since Richardson didn't feel like

FIG 62 - SGT. DAVE RICHARDSON

finishing the run, he stopped and talked to the Green Beret. This was the beginning of his circuitous route that would ultimately lead to him becoming a Green Beret.

After additional intense training he was sent to Vietnam to join Detachment B-52 in January 1969. He received even more training after his arrival and found himself on his first major operation in the middle of April, not on the ground but in the air. Here he was, a couple thousand feet above the A Shau Valley, just a few miles from the Laotion border, manning a radio and listening for reports from the Special Forces recon patrols on the ground. There were just the three of them in the De Havilland Otter (single-engine plane), the pilot, copilot and Dave.

The operation was called Cass Park 1. A major Search and Destroy mission was in the making and the senior mission

FIG 63 - MILITARY OTTER AIRCRAFT

planners wanted intelligence on the number and strength of the enemy forces before committing troops. This was the primary role of Detachment B-52, to conduct long range reconnaissance patrols. Like most of their operations, this mission would last about a month. They deployed from Nha Trang to a FOB (Forward Operating Base) closer to the Area of Operations (AO), which was in this case near Phu Bai. At the end of the mission they would return to Nha Trang to stand down for a week before being assigned their next mission.

There were several recon patrols on the ground that day. Dave's role was to relay transmissions and requests for assistance back to the Forward Operating Base, since the radios with the recon teams on the ground weren't capable of longer range communications. He would also receive regular status reports from the recon teams and relay this information. The group tried to keep a radio relay aircraft in the area over the AO whenever possible when recon teams were on the ground. When a team came into contact with the enemy, the radio relay would usually receive the message first and relay it to the FOB. Men and equipment would be "scrambled" from the FOB and sent to the team in need of assistance. A FAC would also be airborne in the AO and would immediately call in air support if needed.

From Dave's training he knew how the teams were made up, what they carried and how they would react if they encountered an enemy force. Each recon team consisted of six men, three Green Beret noncoms and three South Vietnamese Rangers. The senior Green Beret was in charge.[2] The Americans wanted to blend in with their counterparts. They usually wore the same tiger-striped camouflage fatigues worn by the Rangers. They didn't wear flak jackets or helmets. They didn't want to be identified as Americans if they were observed by the enemy. The men carried AR-15 rifles for the most part. One of the Americans also carried a sawed off M-79 grenade launcher. Of course one of them also carried the radio.

Their equipment could vary, but they carried only the bare necessities. This usually consisted of 500 rounds of ammo, two canteens of water, four fragmentation grenades, two smoke grenades, packages of dried food, a small mirror to attract a helicopter for extraction, a red cloth a couple of feet in diameter which could be used to point out their location on the ground, a poncho and a poncho liner.

April 17, 1969, would turn out to be a busy day. In addition to the recon patrols, other units were also on the ground, including a roadrunner team or two and a South Vietnamese Ranger company. The recon patrols tried to avoid enemy contact. Their role was to observe and they were not equipped to do combat with a large enemy force. The A Shau Valley was a primary point where the North Vietnamese infiltrated South Vietnam, with various parts of the Ho Chi Minh trail just a few miles east of there. The recon patrols were inserted by helicopter for several days at a time. A primary role of the recon patrols was to detect enemy in the area, determine their strength and report what they observed without being detected. The "without being detected" was often difficult, sometimes impossible.

Late in the morning one of the recon teams came into contact with the enemy and called for help, giving their location. One of the Green Berets had already been killed in the action. When they came under attack the three South Vietnamese Rangers turned and fled, leaving the two Americans to fend off an unknown-sized enemy force. One of the surviving Green Berets was wounded and they were in need of immediate help.

Dave relayed the information to the FOB at Phu Bai. The FAC quickly made contact with the recon team and called in air support from available jets. Rangers were sent from the FOB in helicopters to rescue the Americans. Things got worse when the helicopters arrived. A rocket-propelled grenade (RPG) downed the first helicopter on scene, killing the crew. The South Vietnamese Rangers in the other helicopters returned to Phu Bai. A Nung unit was then sent to rescue the Americans. They were able to land and secured the area, getting the Americans out. The Nungs then remained in the area.

FIG 64 - DAVE RICHARDSON IN VIETNAM IN TIGER STRIPES

While the Nungs were being inserted there was a lot of radio traffic. In the midst of this, shortly after noon, Dave heard another voice on the radio. The call sign was covered by other radio traffic, but Dave recognized the voice of a fellow Green Beret, Doug Dahill. Doug was calling for help for his recon team, Recon Team 6. It was a frantic call for help. Dave still remembers Doug's words. "We're in contact! We're running! We have all been hit! If you don't get us out of here before the weather sets in it will be too late!"

The call sign for Team 6 was "Tree Frog". Dave's call sign as relay was "Big Toad". He immediately responded to the call for help, saying "Tree Frog, Tree Frog, this is Big Toad. Do you copy?" At this point the radio operator at the FOB, not having heard the call for help and thinking Dave had the wrong call sign for the action on the ground involving the other team, responded to Dave's message, telling him he was calling the wrong team.

It will never be known if the radio traffic from the FOB cut off a radio response from Dahill and Team 6, but there was no additional radio traffic from the team. Dave transmitted what he had heard to the FOB. Both Dave and the FAC attempted repeatedly to make radio contact, in order to determine their exact location, but there was no response. Assistance was ready and available, but without knowing the location of Team 6, they were of little help. They responded, but without a specific location, they could not find the endangered team as the helicopters flew low over the jungle. Soon the weather closed in and there was no possibility of an extraction.

FIG 65 – SGT. DOUG
DAHILL

FIG 66 – SGT. CHARLES
PREVEDEL

FIG 67 – SGT. CHARLES
NEWTON

The men of Team 6 were never heard from again. A team went in days later in search of the men. They found Viet Cong and engaged them, but didn't find Recon 6. Dave knew two of the Americans, Doug Dahill and Charles Prevedel. He had met Charles Newton, but didn't really know him. Just like that, that quickly, they were gone. He may have met the three South Vietnamese Rangers on the team, but didn't know them.

There would be other battles and other losses in the group while Dave was in Vietnam. At the end of his tour he extended the tour for six months. In fact, his 3-year enlistment had actually ended before he made it home. He was flown back to Fort Lewis, Washington and was immediately discharged, three years and ten days after he had enlisted and 10 days after his enlistment expired. One day he was in the jungles of Vietnam and just a few days later he was not only back in the U.S., but was out of the Army and back in Kansas, a civilian and unprepared for civilian life. This happened to many returning Vets.

Dave enrolled at the University of Kansas and obtained a B.S. degree in electrical engineering. He continued his education while working, obtained an M.S. degree in electrical engineering from the University of Missouri and eventually earned his PhD from Kansas State in 1985. A job assignment took him to Massachusetts in 1987 and he relocated to California in 1990. Along the way he met and married his wife, Kathy and they adopted a daughter, Ashley. Dave and Kathy have five grandchildren. They live in Danville, California. For the past 36 years he has worked in various engineering development projects. He currently belongs to the San Ramon Valley Rotary and the Viet Nam Veterans of Diablo Valley.[3]

During the making of this story Dave learned that his Special Forces buddies who went missing that fateful day were no longer missing. In 1990, the Vietnamese government turned over some bone fragments and other small pieces of evidence that were of U.S. Military origin.

Discussions between the U.S. military and the Vietnamese government subsequently took place resulting in the U.S. government being given permission to excavate the site from where the bone fragments were recovered. There were several trips to Vietnam by teams from JPAC (Joint Prisoner of War/Missing in Action Accounting Command) for site surveys and excavation during the next few years. The

recovered remains were submitted for testing, but it appeared that the remains were all from one person.

JPAC returned for their final excavation in 2006, finding more remains. This ultimately resulted in the identification of all three men. They were finally laid to rest, together, at Arlington National Cemetery, in 2011. The Green Berets of

FIG 68 – DAVE RICHARDSON TODAY

Recon Team Six, call sign "Tree Frog", are finally home.[4]

NOTES AND REFERENCES

[1] A South Vietnamese Ranger company normally consisted of approximately 128 men.

[2] The recon patrols would normally stay in the field for about one week.

[3] The author interviewed Dave Richardson for this story on 5/7/16.

[4] The author received the information on the recoveries of Dahill, Newton and Prevedel directly from Heather Harris, Deputy Director Strategic Partnerships, DPAA (Defense/POW Accounting Agency) on 5/31/16. (This unit has been reorganized and this is the reason for the name change.)

Chapter Fourteen

The Meaning of White Christmas

Michael "Slatts" Slattengren was a typical California teenager when he graduated from Hayward High School in 1964. He was born in Hayward, California and had lived there his entire life. He had one brother and one sister, both younger than him. He enrolled at Hayward State College that fall, living at home and working on his father's poultry farm. The following summer, in 1965, he worked as a firefighter, fighting forest fires. A few months later he received notice in the mail to report for his draft physical.

Slatts didn't really want to be drafted. Draftees in the Army had little or no choice and this didn't appeal to him. Both of his parents had served their country in WWII, his mother in the Army and his father in the Navy. In fact, his father was a Pearl Harbor survivor. His father's service likely influenced his decision to enlist in the Navy. By enlisting he would have some choice and could hopefully learn a trade or skills that could help him in the future. He also looked forward to the possibility of travel, something his father was able to do in the Navy. He took the enlistment oath on

December 28, 1965, shortly after his 19th birthday. The recruiter told him there were no openings in boot camp for a few months, so he was sent home to wait and was finally called up in April 1966.

Fig 69 – MICHAEL "SLATTS" SLATTENGREN

He went to Boot Camp in San Diego and later joined VP 31 (patrol squadron 31) there where he became an Aviation electrician's mate. In August 1968 he was assigned to VP 22, which was an ASW (Anti-Submarine Warfare) squadron, assigned to electrical maintenance on its aircraft. He spent time at Barber's Point, Hawaii with the unit and was deployed to Vietnam on his first tour later that year. He spent his time in Vietnam at the U.S. Naval Air Facility at Cam Ranh Bay.

The primary role of VP 22, even when in Vietnam, was monitoring and tracking Russian submarines, a function of the Cold War. The aircraft also provided patrols for suspicious ships along the South Vietnamese coastline, but this was a secondary role.

Slatts' younger brother, Gary, graduated from high school in 1967. Gary and Slatts corresponded by mail. The draft was in full force by this time and Gary was concerned about this, evidenced by his letters. Slatts suggested to Gary that he enlist in the Navy and request "brother duty", which would allow them to be together. Gary took his advice and enlisted, going to school to become a radio operator. After schooling, Gary was assigned to VP 22 as a radio operator on

P-3 patrol aircraft and they were finally together again in January 1969, at their base in Hawaii. They were bunkmates when stationed there, although their different schedules didn't permit them to spend a lot of time together.

In November 1969 their squadron was deployed to Southeast Asia. The way things worked was that the squadron was on 2-week rotations between three different duty stations. One of the bases was the Naval Station, Sangley Point. Sangley Point is about eight miles southwest of Manila, in the Philippines, in Cavite City. The second station was at the U.S. Naval Air Facility at Cam Ranh Bay, Vietnam. The third station was U-Tapao, Thailand, at the U-Tapao Royal Navy Airfield. Slatts would occasionally see this brother at U-Tapao and at Sangley Point, but they were never together in Vietnam. Whether or not there was any official policy to keep them apart in Vietnam Slatts didn't know, but they were never together there.

Fig 70 – GARY AND SLATTS SLATTENGREN

Slatts often worked nights on the aircraft and there was always plenty of work to be done. He had just finished a 2-week stint at U-Tapao on December 24th and left that evening for Sangley Point on an old C-47 aircraft the squadron used for transportation. He was exhausted when they landed after the 4-hour flight and anxious to get to bed. He finally got to bed around 2AM on Christmas morning and was glad he could sleep in on this holiday. He wasn't at all happy when he was awakened at 6AM by his buddy, "Jaw" Whitehead. He just wanted to sleep, but Jaw told him to get up, that he needed to get ready to go to the orphanage.

He recalled donating money each pay period to the Elsie Gaches orphanage and this was apparently their destination, but he knew next to nothing about it. What he did know was that each pay period when he and his buddies went to get their money, the chaplain was waiting, asking them for a donation for the orphanage. It was hard to refuse the chaplain, so Slatts donated. Now Jaw told him a group of them were going to the orphanage to spend Christmas with the children there.

Tired and a little reluctant, he got up and got ready to go. After washing up and having breakfast, he donned his civilian clothes. They weren't allowed to leave the base in uniform unless they were on duty and they certainly weren't on duty today. The men got into a couple of vans and made their way through Cavite City. This was a poverty-stricken area. It reminded him of the Old West as they drove through the city streets. Here people openly carried guns. It wasn't the safest place off-base. He thought of his family on this most special of holidays and wondered what his parents and sister were doing back in Hayward. He wished his brother could have been at Sangley Point, but it just didn't work out for them to be together. They drove for more than an hour before arriving at the orphanage.

The orphanage was housed in an old villa, donated by an American family, the Gaches. It was somewhat unique in that it wasn't just orphans housed there, but children who were physically and/or mentally disabled, what we would term "special needs" children today. Not all were abandoned by their parents. In some cases the parents simply weren't able to support them.

When the Americans walked in, there were 30 to 40 children waiting for them, of all different ages and with different types of disabilities, some more severe than others. The sailors mingled with the children and staff, getting to know them a bit. At one point the children asked the Americans to sing Christmas carols, so the men gathered in the front of the room, unrehearsed, to honor the request. The song all the children wanted to hear was "White Christmas", so the men sang that song.

Slatts thought about the request for this song. These children had never seen snow and it was unlikely any of them would ever see snow. Many of them were unable to comprehend the concept of snow, yet they wanted to hear this song. Maybe, for the children, it was a symbol of America and what America stood for.

Later the men sat with the children and helped them open Christmas gifts. It was a special time for all. Slatts sat down beside a severely disabled tiny girl who appeared to be about two years old to help her open her gifts. He asked a staff member how old she was and the staff member said she was 21 years old. He couldn't believe that this tiny, child-like girl was actually 21. Such was the extent of her disabilities.

A few hours later it was time to leave. They were thousands of miles away from home, but each had experienced the true meaning of Christmas in this foreign land. None of them would ever forget this experience. For

Slatts, there would be no hesitation when the chaplain came around on pay day.

Fig 71 –JOE "JAW" WHITEHEAD 2ND FROM LEFT, SLATTS 6TH FROM LEFT

His 4-year enlistment was nearing its end in April 1970 and he flew home, arriving at Travis Air Force base. His parents met him there for his homecoming and he rode home with them. Within a week he was discharged and was a civilian once again.

In the summer of 1970, Slatts got a job with Pacific Bell. He also met his future wife, Sue, that year. After his discharge he immediately began growing his hair long, until he could wear it in a ponytail. There was so much animosity in the San Francisco Bay Area toward Vietnam Vets and he didn't want to stand out. He also started attending Hayward State College at night. By this time his hair was long and he wasn't easily singled out as being a Vietnam Vet. [1]

Fig 72 – SLATTS SLATTENGREN TODAY

He married Sue in 1972 and graduated from college in 1975. He and Sue raised three children, two sons and a daughter and currently have five grandsons. Slatts stayed with the phone company through several changes, working his way into management and retired in 2011 from AT&T after 41 years of service. He is an active member of Viet Nam Veterans of Diablo Valley and belongs to VFW Post 75 in Danville, California. Occasionally he still thinks of that Christmas in 1969, a fond memory in a far off land.[2]

NOTES AND REFERENCES

[1] California State College at Hayward has undergone several name changes over the years and is now called California State University East Bay.

[2] Michael Slattengren was interviewed for this story on 3/18/16

Chapter Fifteen

Welcome Home!

Mike Martin is one of those self-made men, someone who managed to overcome early obstacles in life without much help or support. He was born in Phoenix, Arizona and knew virtually nothing about his father. He grew up with his mother and stepdad in a less than ideal situation. His stepdad was career Air Force and a raging alcoholic. They moved around a lot and Mike attended 28 different schools by the time he completed 8th grade and three high schools in three different states. He ran away from home after his junior year in high school and went to Tucson. He moved in with an aunt and grandmother and finished high school there in June of 1965.

He managed to enroll at the University of Arizona immediately after finishing high school. That same week he received his draft notice. Since Mike was already enrolled in college he was able to obtain a 2S student deferment, which was for one year. He knew he wanted to continue his education so he enlisted in the Navy Reserves in order to complete his education and avoid the draft. He knew he wanted to be a naval officer after school so he got accepted to attend the first portion of Officer Candidate School (OCS) in the summer of 1967, between his junior and senior year.

Meanwhile, he was working full-time to pay for his room and board and college fees. Still, with all of this going on, he managed to graduate from college in 1968, a year ahead of schedule. After graduation, he completed the second half of OCS and was commissioned an ensign in the U.S. Navy in the fall of 1968.[1]

After more training Mike was shipped to Vietnam on July 4, 1969. He was assigned to the Naval Support Division at Da Nang and his assignment was in the Freight Operation

Division. His official title was Freight Expedite Officer. He describes his assignment in Vietnam as that of a trucking foreman, in charge of 180 trucks that had off-loaded supplies from ships in the Da Nang harbor and were delivering the supplies all around this part of Vietnam. He was not a combat soldier. He was "behind the wire" as he

Fig 73 - Ensign Mike Martin 1969

calls it. Sure, Da Nang received regular rocket attacks, but he wasn't in the thick of it as so many were. Most of his job was routine and uneventful.

A year later, on July 4, 1970, Mike had been promoted to Lieutenant J.G. (Junior Grade) and had completed his 1-year tour of duty. He was happy to be leaving as he waited at the Da Nang airfield. By all outward appearances, all of the others were just as happy as he was. It was a mixed bag of men who waited to board the TWA commercial jet that would take them home. The uniforms reflected various ranks of Navy, Army and Marine personnel as they stood in line to board the big jet, about 200 happy souls who wanted nothing more than to go home, see their girlfriends or wives and resume a normal life.

There was a lot of boisterous behavior, beginning with loud cheers when the plane lifted off and headed out over the ocean. Loud conversation continued through the long flight home, most of it focusing on girls and drinking and what the men would do when they got home.

After a very long flight home the plane approached L.A. International Airport and entered a landing pattern. The cheers began even before the plane touched down. When the wheels touched the ground there was near pandemonium in the plane with the loud cheers and yells. The men couldn't wait to get off the plane, but somehow they got off in an orderly fashion and entered the terminal. Home on Independence Day! How much better could it get?

The men weren't prepared for what awaited them. All were still in uniform. Mike was wearing his camouflage fatigues. Others wore various uniforms of their branches of service. They were definitely aware of unrest in the U.S. about the war, but didn't expect what happened next.

There were about 150 protestors waiting for them, carrying protest signs, chanting slogans and yelling "baby killer". They stepped in front of the servicemen, blocking their paths when possible. The men weren't ready for this and there were no measures to keep the two groups apart. The Vets kept their composure, much to their credit, side-stepping the protestors and trying to move past them.

As Mike weaved his way through the protestors he saw a young woman in front of him, an attractive young, full-figured gal, still a teenager. He still recalls that she had a peace symbol on a chain around her neck and was wearing typical hippy garb of the day, including sandals. She had a filthy mouth and was yelling obscenities at the returning Veterans. As he stepped to the side to walk around her, she spit at him, hitting him directly in the face. Her action stung, but in ways she could not imagine.

Mike was not a combat soldier. He hadn't killed anyone. He had a total of two hours weapons training and he was "behind the wire" so to speak, in a relatively safe zone. His job was supervising the loading of trucks and delivery of materiel. This girl and her friends were clueless. Many of the men on this plane were draftees and had no choice in the matter, yet all of these men were lumped into one group that she and her companions labeled "baby killers". There were references to "My Lai" on some of the signs. The terminology became increasingly popular after the isolated incident in 1968 when Lt. William Calley, an infantry officer, and some of his men were accused of murdering innocent civilians. The incident became known as the My Lai Massacre and Calley was later convicted of killing innocent villagers. [2]

These were not the same men, though. Many, like Mike, weren't even in combat, but this misinformed bunch of protesters put everyone in the same bag. Mike simply stepped around the woman and walked past her and the others who were trying to block his path.

Mike completed his 4-year obligation in the military at various bases and left the Navy in April 1972. He worked for Xerox for 22 years and then worked in sales for various companies. Mike lives in Castro Valley and has two children and five grandchildren. He is a member of the American Legion and VFW in Castro Valley as well as his local chamber of commerce. He is a commissioner at the Veterans Memorial Building in Hayward. He is one of the founders of the Viet Nam Veterans of Diablo Valley. He and Bill Green head up the Speakers Bureau, which brings knowledge and understanding of the Vietnam War to local students, including the fact that Vietnam Vets weren't a bunch of baby killers.

Fig 74 - Mike Martin today

Mike often reflects on the war and his return home. A most vivid memory of his Vietnam War experience didn't even occur in Vietnam, but at the Los Angeles airport in his own country. He can't help but wonder what happened to that young woman and the other protestors. Did they ever come to the realization of how misguided they were and that their targets should not have been the young men caught up in the war? One can only hope so.[3]

NOTES AND REFERENCES

[1] He was the Distinguished Naval Graduate in his OCS class.

[2] The incident occurred on March 16, 1968, but the public did not become aware of it until late November 1969, when major magazines and the news media broke the story. Trials of several men began in November 1970, so this case remained in the news until the trials were finished in 1971, which may have been an impetus, but not an excuse, for the actions of the protestors.

[3] Mike Martin was interviewed for this story on 10/15/15.

Chapter Sixteen

STAB Boat Stake Out

Dennis Giacovelli just knew he was going to be drafted. It was the summer of 1968 and the 19 year-old college student knew his number was up. There was absolutely no doubt in his mind. Four of his buddies who were attending San Francisco City College with him discussed their options. With the draft looming over their heads they wanted some choice in the matter, so all of them went down to the Navy Recruiting Center and enlisted in the U.S. Navy. He was right about the draft. He received his notice while he was in Boot Camp, so he had made his decision just in time.

After Boot Camp Dennis attended Engineman's School to learn how to repair Navy diesel engines. At graduation the scuttlebutt was that everyone in the class would be assigned to River Patrol Boats (PBR) where the mortality rate was around 50%. Dennis thought that since it was going to be risky anyway, he decided to volunteer for a new unit that was being formed, Strike Assault Boat Squadron 20 (Stabron 20).

For this assignment he received additional small boat training at Mare Island, California.

These STAB boats were aluminum, 24 feet long. They were basically ski boats with a "punch". There were only 22 of them, so it was going to be a small, elite unit. Each boat had twin 427 cubic inch Chevy engines. The engines were housed in heavily insulated compartments. They exhausted beneath the water. This allowed them to operate very quietly and they were fast, capable of speeds of 50+ MPH. They had no canopy so they also sat low in the water and had a low profile. Each boat was filled with Styrofoam from stem to stern to keep it from sinking, regardless of damage.

There was no doubt why this unit was formed or where they were headed after finishing training. Vietnam was their destination and the boats were deemed to be well-suited for the shallow water operations in the Mekong Delta.

FIG 75 - DENNIS GIACOVELLI IN BOOT CAMP

FIG 76 – DENNIS IN VIETNAM

Dennis was the mechanic/engineer on his boat. There were three others, all enlisted men. One was the radio operator who also commanded the boat, the bos'n mate who drove the boat and kept it supplied, and a gunner's mate who was in charge of the weapons and ammo. They all shared the same enlisted rank (E-4).

The boat was equipped with four M60 machineguns, two in gun mounts on either side of the boat, as well as one in the rear and one in the right front. An automatic grenade launcher was on the left front. The boat also had an FM radio for communications. Dennis completed training and was shipped to Vietnam in February 1970. For the first several weeks he was assigned to PBR's (Patrol Boat River) while the boats were being shipped overseas.

The home base of their operations was the USS Benewah, anchored at An Long. The ship served as a floating barracks, with the STAB boats anchored alongside. The crews weren't there very often and spent most of their time on various types of missions, rarely spending more than a day on the mother ship.

Stabron 20 had several responsibilities. They would board and search sampans. They conducted nightly "stake outs", in order to disrupt river crossings. They inserted friendly forces at different points along the rivers in the Mekong Delta and provided fire support during certain types of operations. They engaged in psychologic warfare operations and conducted medical evacuations as necessary for friendly forces.

Their typical mission or operation lasted 5 or 6 days. One of the main roles was intercepting river crossings at night by enemy forces. Normally 6 to 8 boats would participate in these interdiction missions. The boats would operate in pairs. During the daytime they would hang out at an Army base somewhere along a canal. In the late afternoon they would head out and position themselves at various locations along the river, with one boat on each side of the river. Here they would lie in wait for any traffic that tried to move down the river or cross the river at night.

Stabron 20 participated in 31 firefights during the year they were in Vietnam, many of them on these night time interdiction missions. Some were completely uneventful; others were not. Dennis saw both types. He was originally assigned to the #19 boat, call sign "Racing Danger 19" and was later assigned to "Racing Danger 12".

Late one afternoon the Racing Danger crew 12 arrived at their assigned spot, pulling up to the shoreline. In some areas the shoreline was completely clear, without vegetation. This allowed all four of the men to spend the night on the boat, since the shoreline was clearly visible and there was little chance of an ambush. In other places the

FIG 77 - DENNIS WITH HIS M60 MACHINEGUN

area along the shore was covered in heavy vegetation, making it impossible to see just a few feet inland.

This was one of those areas where the crew couldn't see anything inland. Large, thick bushes met the boat when they pulled up against the shore, with an incline rising behind the shoreline. It wasn't a good place to spend the night, but there weren't any options. Dennis and one of the other men on the crew were assigned shore duty. Their job was to protect the boat and intercept any enemy troops who tried to get to the boat.

FIG 78 - STAB BOAT ON THE MEKONG DELTA

Before it got too dark they gathered their gear and moved into the brush, up the incline. They were wearing their fatigues, a long-sleeved shirts, flak jackets, helmets and jungle boots. The stifling heat, humidity and bugs were not their friends, but something with which they had to contend. As they arrived at what they considered a good vantage point, they placed two claymore mines in front of them, which they could detonate from their position. Along with one M60 machinegun they carried from the boat, they each had an M-16 rifle and a revolver. They also carried a Starlight (night vision) scope, a portable radio, two grenades, a grenade launcher and flares.

Back on the boat the two remaining men would take turns staying awake and the same would happen with Dennis and his buddy. It was going to be a hot, uncomfortable night. They quietly settled in, trying to find a reasonably comfortable, or at least acceptable, spot in the brush.

When it was time for Dennis to stand his watch he was miserable and tired. It had already been a long day for all of them. It was quiet in the early morning hours, making it even more difficult to stay awake. All he could see from his vantage point, looking down through the darkness, were miles and miles of rice paddies. As much as he tried to stay alert and awake, fatigue began to overtake him as he stared through the darkness. The M60 was alongside him, as was his M-16. Suddenly he felt a weight on his leg as something touched it! He reached for the M60, but it was facing the wrong direction. He looked down at his leg to see what was on it. To his surprise and relief the enemy turned out to be a huge rat! Its tail was at least 18 inches long. The rat moved off, but it was several minutes before Dennis' heart stopped racing. The rat was lucky to survive the encounter. Needless to say, he had no trouble staying awake for the remainder of the night. This was one of those stories he didn't share with his crew, the VC rat story.

FIG 79 – DENNIS GIACOVELLI, 2ND FROM RIGHT, WITH CREW

Dennis had many other experiences in his year-long tour that weren't so uneventful. Stabron 20 was deactivated on October 20, 1970. and the boats were shipped back to the U.S. Dennis stayed in Vietnam for a few months longer, completed his tour and returned home in February 1971.

When he got out of the Navy Dennis enrolled and later graduated from Heald Engineering College. He began a long career of designing houses and currently owns his own home design business. He is married, has one daughter and lives in Danville, California. Dennis is an active member of Viet Nam Veterans of Diablo Valley.[1]

FIG 80 - DENNIS (CENTER) WITH SOME OF HIS BOAT 19 CREW IN 2010

NOTES AND REFERENCES

[1] Dennis Giacovelli was interviewed for this story on 11/20/15. Some of the background information about Stabron 20 is from a story written by the unit commander, CDR. John Kirk Ferguson.

Chapter Seventeen

Ambush at VC Lake

Rich Lambert is a native Californian. Born in San Francisco, he spent most of his youth in San Jose and Los Gatos, moving to Coalinga with his family for his junior high and high school years. After high school he enrolled at U.C. Santa Barbara. During his senior year he received notice to report for his draft physical. Fortunately, he was deferred until he graduated.

After graduation he moved back to Coalinga. He applied to both the Navy and Air Force flight programs. He heard from the Navy first, so that became his choice. He completed AOCS (Aviation Officer Candidate School), a 16-week course and was commissioned an Ensign. Rich went on to flight school and received his "Wings of Gold", qualifying him as a naval aviator and then received additional training to become a helicopter pilot.

It was September 1969 when Rich arrived in Vietnam, assigned to HA(L)3 Light Attack Helicopter Squadron 3), the

Seawolves. Rich was originally assigned to be a "slick" pilot, flying the troop-carrying and equipment-carrying Hueys. Initially, he flew several missions with the Army as a copilot, flying Medevac missions, picking up wounded and transporting them to hospitals and ferrying replacement aircraft. This soon changed and he found himself assigned to Detachment 1, getting in-country gunship training.

There were nine detachments of Seawolves in the Mekong Delta when Rich arrived. Rich was assigned to Detachment 1 at Seafloat/Solid Anchor on the Ca Mau Peninsula.

The outlying detachments were small, with two helicopters assigned to each. There were eight pilots and eight crewmen assigned to each detachment, comprising four crews. The crews were on alert 24 hours at a time, so every other day they had a 24-hour shift. Some of the time they flew at night, with all Seawolves being rated IFR, capable of night flying.[1]

FIG 81 - LT JG RICH LAMBERT

His early missions were flown as a copilot and, after gaining combat experience, he was moved up to first pilot or AHAC (Attack Helicopter Aircraft Commander). Many of the missions were in support of SEAL teams, but he also flew missions supporting the Brown Water Navy and psy ops (psychological operations) missions, dropping leaflets urging the Viet Cong to surrender and switch sides.

There was one particularly disappointing mission where they were just too late. Intelligence information was developed that some Americans were being held prisoner by the Viet Cong and a SEAL team was immediately sent to attempt to free them. Rich's crew flew in support of the mission. When the team arrived and landed, there were fires still burning at the camp, but the enemy and the prisoners were gone. They had missed them by just hours.

The support missions continued into 1970. They were also supporting the river patrol boats in the region and responded to attacks on the boats, as well as occasional missions when the Vietnamese Army (ARVN) and the U.S. Army needed help. By early September he was nearing the end of his tour and looking forward to going home. On September 15th of that year, his crew was called to assist an Army helicopter on the Cau Mau peninsula, at a place called VC Lake. It got its name from the large numbers of encounters with the Viet Cong near this lake.

The reason for the call was that an Army Medevac Huey, Dust Off -86, had run into heavy fire when it tried to evacuate six wounded ARVN soldiers from along VC Lake. The South Vietnamese Army had unexpectedly encountered a much larger Viet Cong force there, supported by the North Vietnamese Army. Several troops were wounded and an urgent call went out to evacuate the most seriously wounded. Dust Off -86, flown by Army 1st Lt. Kenneth Ledford, attempted to make the rescue, but the intense fire directed at him on his approach made it impossible for him to land. He needed gunships to suppress the fire, so he backed off.[2]

There were no Army gunships available to assist in suppressing the enemy fire and facilitate the evacuation, so Ledford called for help from the Navy and Seawolves "scrambled" to assist.[3]

The other Detachment 1 helicopter at Ca Mau was down for maintenance so one of the Hueys from Detachment 3, flown by Lt. Baratko, was called to assist. Rich's chopper and the one from Detachment 3 responded. In addition, two gunships from Detachment 6 were also scrambled.

The plan was for the four Navy gunships to cover the Army helicopter when it landed to pick up the wounded, suppressing the fire coming from the NVA and VC troops on the ground. The gunships would lead the way, raking the surrounding area with fire. The Army helicopter would come in behind the gun ships to retrieve the wounded. Rich's Huey and the others would make firing passes on both sides of the evacuation area as the Army helicopter landed, and peel off and continue to make passes until the Army Huey had picked up the wounded, taken off and was safely out of the immediate area.[4]

It was a simple plan, but it didn't work. As soon as the helicopters began their initial descent, they were met by intense ground fire from all directions, both small arms and .51 caliber fire. It was clearly a trap. All four Seawolves were hit with small arms and heavy weapons fire. Bill Pederson, flying the lead helicopter from Detachment 6, was hit the worst and immediately started to go down. He was directly over the landing zone. The helicopter hit hard and rolled onto its side on a dike in a rice paddy.

Lt. David Speidel's helicopter, the other Huey from Detachment 6, was hit and severely damaged, with the rudder controls knocked out. Speidel was barely able to keep the Huey airborne and immediately left, limping back to his base. Dust Off -86, seeing the other helicopters get hit with the murderous fire, abandoned his landing approach and left the immediate area.

Rich and Bill Pederson were buddies, having trained together at S.E.R.E (Survival, Evasion, Resistance, Escape) school together, both were from California and were sent to Vietnam at the same time. Rich was beginning his circling cover tactic with Pederson, covering Dust Off -86, when he too was hit by heavy .51 caliber fire. The engine was hit and stopped and the helicopter began to go down.

This was a bad situation. Rich observed they were going down right on top of the enemy. He had little altitude and the helicopter was in auto rotation. He quickly realized it was better to take their chances landing in the lake than in the middle of the enemy force as he put out a Mayday call while the Huey descended. He had no idea how deep the water was, but it was still better than landing in the middle of the enemy. Somehow he managed to maneuver the helicopter over the water. As this was happening Rich still took time to say a quick prayer, "Lord, if you get me out of this one I'll be a good guy the rest of my life." The Huey had a tendency to roll on its side during an auto rotation landing due to the torque forces, but Rich's landing was perfect and the helicopter

181

splashed down and settled into the lake upright. Fortunately, the water was only about 4-feet deep.[5]

They immediately began taking small arms fire from the shoreline with the water churning up around the downed aircraft. The crew began removing equipment and Rich quickly removed the four screws that attached the black box (containing radio gear) to the console and pulled it out. The crew chief/door gunner, Dave Smale, climbed onto the roof to secure the rotor blade, tying it out of the way to make it safe for the crew to climb on the roof alongside him. Rich and the rest of the crew climbed onto the roof of the gunship. They were still in serious trouble, taking fire from the shoreline.[6]

Meanwhile, the only gunship still flying had also been badly hit. The pilot, Lt. Baratko, smelled the strong odor of fuel in his cockpit and knew he had a leak somewhere. Since he was the only gunship still in the air, if he left, there was no chance the men in the downed helicopters could be rescued by the Army Huey without fire support. With this in mind, Baratko made a conscious decision to stay and provide support for the others as long as possible.

Standing on the roof of the Huey with his crew, Rich looked up and saw Dust Off -86 coming across the water. The ground fire intensified as the helicopter tried to hover near them. The chopper aborted its first attempt, due to the intensity of the enemy fire, circled and came around again. Rich could see the splashes all around him from the enemy bullets hitting the water. On this pass the Army chopper hovered above them and he and his men quickly climbed onto the skids and into the helicopter.[7]

Lt. Ledford was anxious to get out of the area, but Rich knew there was still the possibility that some of Pederson's crew had survived their crash. Once inside, Rich got a headset plugged it into the intercom system and, standing behind Ledford's seat, told him they couldn't leave without checking for survivors in the other downed helicopter. Ledford was understandably reluctant to brave the murderous fire again. Rich told him he'd fly the Huey if Ledford didn't feel up to it. With no one else available to attempt a rescue, Ledford agreed and maneuvered his helicopter back toward the wreckage on the ground. They received heavy fire from tree lines on both sides of the dikes and beyond as they descended. Above them, Lt. Baratko made repeated passes over the area with his gunship, while both door gunners raked the area with their fire from their machineguns. Ledford set down near the crash site.

Rich had brought his M-16 rifle and M79 grenade launcher with him, two items he took with him from the crashed Huey and always had with him in the helicopter. He began firing his M-16 from the open doorway in the direction the fire was coming from, then stopped briefly to fire a few rounds from the grenade launcher. Rich's door gunners, Smale and White, were also firing their M-16's. Copilot Mike Lagow waded through the water in the rice paddy to the wreckage to check for survivors. He was accompanied by crew chief Mitchell from Dust Off -86. Small arms and machinegun fire rounds were hitting the ground all around the helicopter as soon as it landed, as well as mortar shells bursting nearby as the enemy tried to zero in on them.

Lagow found Pederson unresponsive, trapped in the pilot's seat. The copilot was also wedged in his seat, badly wounded, but alive. Lagow finally freed the copilot and began carrying him back to Dust Off -86. Mitchell found door gunner Plona badly wounded alongside the wreckage. Mitchell helped him up and they stumbled through the water toward the waiting helicopter, falling along the way. Smale stopped firing his M-16 and went to the wreckage to assist. He found the other door gunner, Ramos, dead alongside the wreckage. Smale saw Lagow carrying the wounded copilot and went to assist him.[8]

Meanwhile, Rich exited the helicopter and made his way through the water to help get the two injured men back to the chopper and check on the two other crew. He looked in the cockpit and found his friend Bill Pederson trapped in the twisted wreckage, unresponsive and clearly deceased, as was the other crewman, door gunner Ramos. Confirming both were dead, Rich returned to Dust Off -86 before it lifted off.[9]

They flew to Binh Thuy with the two wounded Seawolves, gunner Jim Plona and copilot Bill Ford. These men were taken to the 3rd Surgical Hospital for treatment of their wounds. Miraculously, none of Rich's crew was wounded on the mission.[10]

Rich's yearlong tour was nearly at an end and he returned to the U.S. later that month. Upon his return, he received training in ASW (Anti-Submarine Warfare) and was assigned to HS-4 (Helicopter Anti-Submarine Squadron 4) aboard the USS Ticonderoga. Rich was released from active duty in 1973. He remained in the Naval Reserves, eventually retiring in April 1995 with the rank of Captain after 27 years of service.

When released from active duty Rich became a commercial realtor, where he still works today. He and his wife Katarina have two adult daughters and live in Walnut Creek, California. He is an active member and former

President of the Viet Nam Veterans of Diablo Valley and is also active in his church.[11]

FIG 82 - RICH LAMBERT TODAY

NOTES AND REFERENCES

[1] Some, but not all Army pilots were rated IFR.

[2] The information about the number of ARVN soldiers wounded and other specific information is from Lt. Ledford's Navy Cross Citation.

[3] Lt. Kenneth Ledford was in the 58th Medical Battalion, 68th Medical Group.

[4] Rich recalled seeing only his helicopter, Pederson's helicopter and Ledford's helicopter at the time he was shot down. Army Specialist Mike Mitchell's Silver Star Citation and Lt. j.g. Baratko's Citation both reference four helicopters in the area at that time, so I've used that information in the story.

[5] Rich explained he practiced auto-rotational landings whenever he had the opportunity. The training and practice obviously paid off. He also described this

landing as the best auto-rotational landing he ever made.

[6] The black box was a small box containing coded radio gear.

[7] The Silver Star citation for Army Specialist Mike Mitchell, gunner/crew chief on the helicopter piloted by Ledford, references that his helicopter couldn't make the rescue on its first pass and had to come around again. Rich Lambert didn't specifically recall that the Army helicopter was forced to make a second pass.

[8] The remains of Pederson and Ramos were later removed by U.S. Navy forces.

[9] The accounts differed slightly as to what each of the men on Rich Lambert's crew were doing when the rescue was made, but all were engaged in some aspect of the rescue. The author relied on excerpts from the book *Fire in the Sky* (pp 151-159) for clarification on some of the sequence of events for the rescue itself as well as Rich's Bronze Star citation.

[10] Both were severely wounded and were sent back to the U.S. for treatment.

[11] Rich Lambert's personal account of this story resulted from interviews with the author on 3/16/16, 9/7/16 and 2/27/17.

Chapter Eighteen

Beyond the Front Lines

Not everyone who was in Vietnam experienced firsthand combat. Some witnessed the results of war from a relatively safe area, although the entire country was still a war zone and no area was completely safe. One of these men was Don Schroeder. Don spent his tour in Vietnam at the 95th Evacuation Hospital in Da Nang, a Mobile Army Surgical Hospital (M.A.S.H.)

Don was born in Brooklyn, New York and grew up in Garden City on Long Island. He graduated from Chaminade High School in Mineola, New York. After that he attended St. Bonaventure in Olean, New York and earned a Bachelor's Degree.

On February 12, 1968, Don began his first job after college at the Springs Mills in New York City, a leader in the textile industry. Oddly enough, he received his draft notice that same day. He continued working until his induction on May 6th of that year. Draftees had a 2-year commitment, often with little or no choice as to assignment. Don found himself in this position. An opportunity presented itself for Don to get additional training, something he might possibly use later in life. He could be trained in mental hygiene but this required a third year of service. He signed up for that extra year and was trained as a psychiatric technician.

After training, Don had received orders to report for assignment with the 3rd Armored Division in Germany, so he went home and married his girlfriend Jean. His job there was primarily interviewing and assessing soldiers with drug and psychiatric issues. Within a few months he received orders for Vietnam. After a trip home he flew to Vietnam, arriving there in January 1970.

On arrival, he landed at the airfield at Long Binh. Just landing there was a frightening experience as the men getting off the plane were quickly loaded onto buses with wire mesh on the windows, while rockets or shells were exploding around the perimeter of the airfield. It was quite a welcome to the war. Don got off the bus in a holding area and subsequently boarded a plane that took him to Da Nang, to the 95th Evacuation Hospital, which would be his new home.

This hospital treated a variety of patients, including U.S. Army and Marines, South Vietnamese (ARVN) troops, along with Vietnamese civilians that showed up at the hospital. In fact, Don estimates that 50% of the patients treated there were civilians in need of medical assistance. Some of the Vietnamese had war-related injuries, but others were treated for diseases and other ailments. Mothers came to the hospital to have their babies born and they even treated Viet Cong and NVA wounded as well, who were always guarded by American troops.

One of Don's primary assignments was doing an initial assessment of those who came to the hospital for psychiatric treatment. Based on Don's assessment, he would refer the patient to a psychiatrist, a psychologist or a social worker. Don did more than 100 such assessments during his time in Vietnam. One might think that most of the patients were suffering from a condition connected directly to combat, but that wasn't the case. The majority of the patients he saw came in with a condition unrelated to the war.

Family issues going far back to childhood were commonplace. A few came in despondent over a "Dear John" letter and others came in with heroin addiction problems. There was even a patient who came in after having a bad LSD experience, having received the LSD from a girlfriend. The issues were many and varied.

Fig 83 - Vietnamese boy at Evac Hospital

Don also did duty as an orderly in the psychiatric ward, and often during the night time hours he worked in both the psychiatric and dermatology wards. If help was needed elsewhere in the hospital everyone pitched in, regardless of primary assignment. This was especially true with incoming wounded. Ninety per cent of the combat casualties came in at night. The frequency of wounded coming in at night was unpredictable and there was generally less staffing during the evening hours.

Typically, Don would be working in the psych or dermatology ward when someone from admitting would run in, saying there were incoming wounded and assistance was needed. Don and others would quickly make their way out to the helicopter pad. He never knew what awaited him and couldn't see through the darkness into the helicopter. Screams and moans would let him know the patient was still alive. He and others would load the wounded onto stretchers and carry them into the hospital where doctors and nurses would take over. It was a simple assignment, but not an easy one.

Fig 84 - Medevac Huey at 95th Evac Hospital

U.S. military troops had two dog tags in Vietnam. The infantrymen often wore one dog tag on a chain around their neck and the other tied to one of their boot laces. One night he was called to assist with wounded. It was dark and Don really couldn't see very much inside the helicopter that just landed. One of the medics, a sergeant, told Don to retrieve the dog tag off a wounded soldier's boot lace. Through the darkness Don went to remove the dog tag, but the soldier's leg was missing. That memory isn't easy to forget.

Another night Don was on duty in the psych ward. As he was going about his normal routine he saw a patient walking toward him, a big guy. He saw the soldier was agitated, talking. The man was obviously upset, talking louder and approached Don, calling him a VC. Don looked closely and saw the soldier had a pair of scissors in his hand as he approached. The patient was clearly experiencing some kind of a psychotic episode and this was not a safe situation. Don, as calmly as possible, told the patient that he wasn't a VC, he was an American. He doesn't recall the exact words he said, but after a few tense minutes he was able to persuade the soldier to lay down the scissors. He walked the patient back to his bed and the patient was given a shot of Thorazine, an anti-psychotic drug to keep him calm the rest of the night.

Fig 85 - Don Schroeder (far right) at China Beach

Despite the work load, it wasn't all work and no play. Although there was plenty of work to do at the hospital, on the occasional day off Don was able to relax. China Beach, made famous by the 1980's TV program, was nearby and was a favorite place for the hospital staff. Don also tended bar in the officer's club at night when he wasn't working.

Don returned to the U.S. in December 1970. He was released early from the Army soon after he returned home. He went to work for Springs Mills again and returned to school to get an MBA from St. Johns University in Queens, NY. In 1974 he transferred to St. Louis and then to San Francisco in 1979. He worked in sales for various textile companies after moving to California and retired in 2012.

Along the way Don and Jean raised three daughters and now have five grandchildren. They live in Alamo, California.[1]

Fig 86 - Don and Vietnam buddy Bob Fraser

NOTES AND REFERENCES

[1] The author interviewed Don Schroeder for this story on 1/3/17

Chapter Nineteen

A Shattered American Dream

It was late morning when the two young men approached the front door of the southern California ranch-style house. This wasn't the first time they had this task. They had done it many times and one would think the repetition would make it easier, but it didn't work that way. In fact, each time was more difficult.

Both wore the uniforms of U.S. Marines, 1st Lt. Thomas Corbett and the sergeant accompanying him wearing their dress tans. Both looked sharp, a requirement for this special assignment. Parked at the curb was their white, unmarked pool van. In 1971 it wasn't popular to be driving around in a vehicle that had any reference to the U.S. military stenciled on it. It was better not to draw unnecessary attention to themselves as they drove through the streets from Camp Pendleton to their suburban destination. The uniforms were where they drew the line, though. They were still Marines and proud of their service to their country, even if some others didn't appreciate it. They were also respectful of their comrades in arms. Still, they sometimes wore windbreakers over their uniforms while driving, taking them off when they exited the car. They wanted no confrontations as they drove through the streets.

Corbett had hoped for a duty assignment in California when he left Vietnam. In fact, he had actually extended his 13-month tour with a vague promise that he'd get a good assignment in the U.S. if he did so. Camp Pendleton was about as far across the country from the Bronx, where he grew up, as he could get. No more cold winters for this New Yorker.

The 26 year-old Marine grew up with four older sisters in a very Catholic family. His uncle was a Jesuit priest. Tom attended parochial school and enrolled in a Jesuit university after high school, the only one of five children to attend college. He later transferred to, and graduated from, the University of Hartford, Connecticut. While in college he and a couple of buddies decided to enlist in the U.S. Navy Reserves, not to avoid the draft or combat, but hoping to serve together.

After graduating from college, Tom found himself on a North Atlantic cruise in the bowels of a smelly supply ship and decided that the Navy wasn't for him. He wondered what combat would be like and decided to apply for a transfer from the Navy to the Marine Corps. After serving as an enlisted man in the Navy he wanted to be an officer and applied for Marine Officer Candidate School. In addition to being an officer, he hoped to become a helicopter pilot. He survived OCS, but eye problems and combat escalations in Vietnam kept him from becoming a pilot. Instead, he became a Marine infantry platoon leader.

After Tom completed advanced infantry training, he was assigned to a pre-deployment training unit at Camp Pendleton, California. Soon he was the only officer on a plane with 230 Marines, destination South Vietnam. They arrived late at night and were welcomed on arrival at the Da Nang airfield with a rocket and mortar attack. The

FIG 87 - LT. THOMAS CORBETT

civilian chartered plane landed without landing lights, stopping at the end of the runway just long enough to off-load its human cargo and then made a quick turnaround to take-off.

Tom hung around the bustling Da Nang base for a few days waiting for assignment to a unit. During this time he recalled a warning during a briefing a few days before he left for Vietnam, that rookie 2nd lieutenants or "brown bars" as they were called, lasted on average just 30 days in Vietnam before they were killed or wounded. Of course he knew in his own mind that this may have happened to others, but wouldn't happen to him. His assignment finally came through, to an MP (Military Police) battalion. Here he was, an infantry officer in Vietnam, trained as a platoon leader, assigned to an MP battalion. Officially he was now a member of the 3rd MP Battalion, Fleet Marine Force (FMF) WESTPAC (Western Pacific).

Now that he had been given his assignment, he was driven to his new base, several miles outside Da Nang. It was the first week of September, 1969. He was headed for Hill 327, known by his fellow Marines as "Monkey Mountain", due to the large number of monkeys living on the hill. The hill was also called "Freedom Hill", because it was one of the last sights Marines saw as they left the airfield at Da Nang on their way home.

His new company commander, Captain Bernard McDermott III, was in the vehicle with him. McDermott was a real gung-ho Marine, the kind of guy you read about in adventure stories. He had recently volunteered for his second tour and was a Force Reconnaissance Marine. McDermott wasn't at all happy to be assigned to an MP unit. He returned to Vietnam to be a fighting Marine, not a guard and insisted to be sent to "the bush", where the heaviest fighting was occurring. His comments had already gained the attention of a Marine colonel, who told him to keep his mouth shut and report as ordered. As they drove down the road a few stray shots rang out. McDermott, totally unfazed, just grinned as he glanced back at Tom in the backseat.

Some of the frontline troops considered the base "the rear" and relatively safe. After all, among other things it had a brig for Marines who had gotten themselves in serious trouble, a POW compound for North Vietnamese officers and a company of scout and sentry dogs and their handlers. The infantry "grunts" of the battalion would escort truck convoys headed up to the DMZ, ran mostly night patrols and were responsible for base perimeter security.

Within days of their arrival, on the night of September 6, 1969, the base at Hill 327 was attacked by the NVA. Mortars and rockets rained down inside the camp. Forty two Marines were wounded that night in the attack and two were killed. One was Captain McDermott, who never got that opportunity to join a recon unit. It was a stark reminder that no place was safe in Vietnam.[1]

FIG 88 - LT. CORBETT READY FOR PATROL

Tom survived the night, collecting only a couple of minor shrapnel wounds. After seeing the carnage, the death and injuries to so many of his men, he couldn't bring himself to report his injuries, but just patched himself up. Twenty years later a piece of that shrapnel would be removed in an emergency room in California. [2]

He was still a platoon leader and led patrols into the surrounding areas, often setting up ambushes. The night patrols were the worst, but he survived his time at Hill 327. He saw some of the countryside, too, escorting truck convoys loaded with supplies up Highway 1 to different outposts. There were bad times and a few good times. Some of the worst times were writing letters to families of his Marines who were killed or wounded. One of the better times was over the Christmas holidays in 1969 when Tom was assigned to provide security for the Bob Hope Christmas tour when it came to Da Nang. He was on the same helicopter as some of the ladies, including Miss World 1969, a nice temporary reprieve from combat.

FIG 89 - TOM CORBETT WITH SCOUT DOG

Late in 1970 his battalion transferred back to the U.S. Tom had served in various assignments, becoming a company commander and finally the Battalion Operations Officer. He stayed on in various capacities, ranging from a temporary assignment working with some CID (Criminal Investigations Division) people to an assignment with Army Intelligence near the DMZ, testing and experimenting with laser sighting devices, which were still secret at that time. Finally, it was his time to return home, with the promise of a good assignment. He was now a 1st lieutenant and would soon be a captain, having been promoted once since his days as a 2nd lieutenant.

The assignment was good, Weapons Training Officer at Marine Corps Recruit Depot, San Diego, attached to Weapons Training at Camp Pendleton. In fact, it was a great assignment. The drill instructors were some of the best he had served with, with little need for supervision. He was called in one day though, and given an additional assignment, that of Notification Officer.

When Marines were killed or seriously wounded enough to be evacuated in Vietnam, the Marine Corps sent a team of one officer and one non-commissioned officer to make the notification to family. Unlike WWII, when most of the notifications were made by telegram, the military decided that these notifications needed to be made in person. Tom didn't want the assignment, but Marines followed orders.

There was no training for this job. Tom had experienced combat, but tough as it was, having to make these notifications was worse. Initially, Tom was given a pamphlet that the Army used as a guide. Occasionally the family had already received notification from Vietnam of the death or injury, but most of the time families were unaware of the situation.

It was on-the-job training. Experience taught him to make notifications during the daytime, whenever possible. He learned to scout the neighborhood before stopping in front of the house. With all the anti-war feelings, he wanted to avoid a confrontation and it was better if neighbors didn't see them. He learned never to stop, but to return later, if small children were in front of the house. Although children obviously wouldn't be given the notification, children of Marines were always happy to see other Marines. Children always asked lots of questions and it was tougher on everyone if children were present. Sometimes children were inside though, and he couldn't control that situation. It was simply heart-wrenching when a little boy or girl answered and ran to tell "Mommy" that some Marines, just like Daddy, were at the door. He learned to always carry smelling salts, to revive family members who felt faint. It was a common happening.

Most of the time the next of kin, whether it was a mother, father or wife, knew the reason for the visit. Whether they saw it on his face or were aware of the policy of personal notifications, they seemed to know. This didn't necessarily make it any easier, but at least they understood the reason for the visit. There was a formal statement that he was supposed to read to the family, expressing regrets on behalf of the President of the United States and the U.S. Marine Corps, ending by thanking the family. He rarely read this statement. It was formal and impersonal. These families didn't need to hear impersonal condolences read from a card.

The families always wanted to know how their loved one died. Sometimes Corbett knew the details, but he never shared the details with the family at that time. The Marine had died a hero, period, regardless of the circumstances and this is what he shared. The family could learn the details later. Not all the Marines died in combat. War zones are not pretty and some died in tragic accidents or were killed by friendly fire or even by drug overdoses or suicides, but the families could learn about this later.

It was a hot day in Riverside, California, when Tom rang the doorbell and waited for someone to answer. They had already scouted the lower middle class neighborhood before they stopped at the small home with the neat yard. This family took pride in the care of their home. As Tom waited for someone to answer, he looked around him for potential problems.

He had a minimal amount of information on the family, but knew the Marine who died was adopted at an early age by a Hungarian family and the adoptive parents were the next of kin. The family had emigrated to the U.S. and to California shortly after the 1956 uprising in Hungary. He knew the son was an only child, but didn't know whether the parents had previous knowledge of the death.

A middle-aged woman answered the door and he asked if he could speak to her. She invited the Marines into the home, speaking with a strong Eastern European accent. A middle-aged man, also with an accent, later determined to be the father, came into the room. Both were small in stature. By the sad expression on his face Corbett saw that this man understood the reason for the visit. Tom introduced himself and his Marine companion to both of them.

As Tom looked around the living room, his eyes caught sight of the mantle. On the mantle above the fireplace stood a long row of photos, the ones on the left showing a small, smiling boy. The series of photos depicted the history of a boy, a happy boy, growing up. There were photos of him in his baseball uniform and football uniform, smiling at the camera. As the photos continued from left to right, one saw the chronology of a boy growing to manhood, including a photo of him in his cap and gown at high school graduation. The last photo on the mantle was the photo of a serious-looking young Marine in his dress blue uniform, obviously taken at boot camp.

As Tom looked around the house he saw the pride. The home was clean and neat. What was unusual about this home was that even the walls were decorated with photos of their son at various times in his life.

Tom never engaged in small talk. He was there for a reason and now he quietly explained how sad it was for him to be there, having to bring them news that their son was killed in Vietnam days earlier. The mother didn't understand or wouldn't accept the news, as the father looked sadly at him. Tom told her again that her son was killed in Vietnam. Finally the realization set in. She started sobbing, as only a mother could, collapsing on the couch. The father moved over to comfort her, now also sobbing. Tom and his partner stood quietly, giving them time.

By one knock on a door and a few words he had destroyed the American dreams of these proud immigrants. When the situation had calmed, Tom explained they would be contacted by other Marines, with information about bringing their son home and assisting with burial arrangements and he provided them with a packet of contact information. The parents still sat on the couch, holding each other, grieving quietly as Tom left. During the notification there was the constant reminder of this young man's life, a childhood filled with joy and hope, which abruptly ended in Vietnam, like it had for so many others, including some of Tom's men.

Whether this notification was worse than the others or whether there was a cumulative effect, he had given just one too many notifications. The notifications were always heart-wrenching. With each notification there was a sensation of profound sadness, not just for the Marine, but for those who loved him.

No one could handle this assignment indefinitely. Tom never counted the number of notifications to parents, wives, children and siblings of fellow Marines. While the Marine Corps wanted the notifications made by Marines who had been in combat, it wasn't easy for Marines who had lost buddies in Vietnam to be given this assignment on their return home. In each case he planned to keep in touch with the families of these Marines, but it was too difficult. He didn't keep in touch with any of them. Tom spoke to his commanding officer, who understood and relieved him of notification duty. It was not a long term assignment, for obvious reasons.

Tom left the Marine Corps in 1972, after 5+ years in the military, anxious to return to civilian life, grow his hair long and blend in. Several years later he wanted to try out for the ski team at Lake Tahoe and needed to have a physical exam. During the exam his doctor found a lump on his throat. The lump led to a diagnosis of Stage 4 throat and thyroid cancer.[3]

He was numb at the diagnosis. He was offered an opportunity to participate in a medical study sponsored by two major universities. The participants in the study were former servicemen who developed various types of cancer after being exposed to Agent Orange, a chemical defoliant used widely in Vietnam. This experimental study was to determine whether or not Agent Orange caused cancer. In return for participating in the study, nearly all expenses for years of treatments and several surgeries would be taken care of by the two medical centers. Tom gladly accepted and, after several surgeries, accompanied by chemo-therapy and radiation, he made a significant recovery. The study determined Tom's cancer most likely resulted from numerous exposures to Agent Orange .[4]

Tom worked in sales for much of his life after he left the military, working in commercial real estate and selling Mercedes Benz automobiles in the San Francisco Bay Area for nearly 20 years. Today he is semi-retired and works as Veterans Liaison Officer for the Oakmont Cemetery in Lafayette, California.

FIG 90- TOM CORBETT TODAY

He is a member of the Third Thursday Veterans Lunch Group, an informal group of Veterans that meets monthly, a member of the Marine Corps Combat Officer's Association, a member of the Marine Corps League and on the board of directors of MOAA (Military Officers Association of America). Tom is currently the liaison between the local high school Jr. ROTC program and MOAA. He is also a member of the Viet Nam Veterans of Diablo Valley and he and his wife, Sidney, live in Martinez, California.[5]

NOTES AND REFERENCES

[1] Source of information: National Archives-Command Chronology Report, 3rd Military Police Battalion, Combat Chronology 1 Sept 1969-30 Sept 1969

[2] In addition, he felt it wouldn't look good in his personnel file for an officer to report being wounded in the buttocks so soon after his arrival.

[3] Stage 4 is the most serious stage of cancer. The survival rate of Stage 4 throat and thyroid cancer in those years was extremely low.

[4] The study, according to Corbett, lasted for 20 years. He was one of the few who survived the entire length of the study and has survived several bouts of

other types of cancer. In the late 70's Vietnam Vets began filing claims for disabilities sustained when exposed to Agent Orange. It was a difficult, nearly impossible battle with the V.A. in the early years, but this has changed somewhat. Corbett never filed a claim with the Veterans Administration and has never sought treatment or compensation through the V.A. for the disabling effects of Agent Orange. Like many Vietnam Vets Tom he has feelings of distrust over experiences when he returned home.

[5] Tom Corbett was interviewed for this story on 2/19/15 and 10/15/15.

Chapter Twenty

"I Want to Go Home"

The two men sat there together, talking quietly at times and at other times seemingly lost in thought. They sat on the sea wall at Fort Point, beneath the first arch of the Golden Gate Bridge on San Francisco Bay. It was a balmy evening, before sunset and the Bay was calm. This was unusual weather. Normally it was cold, with the waves lapping against the sea wall. On this night the weather was perfect.

The year was 1987. Finally the older man spoke, looking through the arches out toward the Pacific Ocean. He spoke of a happy day, of sailing beneath the Golden Gate Bridge and returning home from the Pacific at the end of WWII.

The older man's story prompted the younger man to tell his own story of coming home from a different war, of flying over the Golden Gate Bridge in a chartered Braniff Airways passenger jet on his return from Vietnam, the "Freedom Bird" as they called it, and of the pilot saying over the intercom "Welcome home boys!" After a brief pause the pilot followed up with "Errr, make that welcome home MEN!" Cheers arose from the happy Vets, who jumped up from their seats, cheering, yelling and slapping each other on their backs. A few minutes later they landed at Travis Air Force Base. They were finally home, survivors. Ironically, the pilot's welcome was one of the few that many of these men would ever receive.

After they told their stories both were quiet again. These were special, reflective moments for both. They were enjoying each other's company, particularly so when they weren't talking about their "connection" to each other.

They could have been father and son, but they weren't. The older man, Art Muehe, was indeed a father, the father of Mark Muehe, who was killed in an ambush in faraway Vietnam on December 5, 1969. The younger man was Jim Hardy, who served with Mark in Vietnam. Neither would forget that date, for different reasons, but they were connected in yet another way.

Jim came from a military family. His father was career Navy and was at Pearl Harbor when the first bombs fell in December 1941. Jim was born in Pendleton, Oregon, but moved around a lot growing up. Such was the life when your father was a Naval Officer. Some of his favorite memories are of surfing with his friends in Hawaii, Baja California and Coronado, California, during his high school and college years.

After high school Jim enrolled at San Diego State College, majoring in art. After three years he felt he needed a break. The buildup for the Vietnam War was also starting and he wanted no part of it. So he dropped out of school in 1965 and moved to Paris. He wanted to study art there, but the language was a problem and he wouldn't be allowed to enroll at the Ecole des Beaux Arts without being able to demonstrate a very basic understanding of the French language. So he enrolled at the Sorbonne for several months to study French. He learned enough of the language to be accepted at the Ecole des Beaux Arts after four months. He enjoyed his time in Paris, studying art and meeting new people.[1]

While at the Sorbonne, he befriended two Vietnamese students, a North Vietnamese girl and her South Vietnamese boyfriend. He was even invited to, and attended, a North Vietnamese ball celebrating Tet, the Vietnamese New Year. How ironic it was that their two countries were engaged in a civil war, yet their friendship remained and within three years Jim would be caught up and actively engaged in combat in this same war.

After a year in Paris, he received a terse letter from his uncle, his Uncle Sam that is, strongly urging him to return home to remain in good standing with his local draft board. Jim considered staying in Paris or even moving to neutral Sweden. He didn't want to become involved in the Vietnam War. He also knew his father would disown him if he dishonored the family in this fashion, so he reluctantly said goodbye to his friends and returned to California. He was able to defer his service until he completed his Bachelor of Arts degree and was then inducted into the Army on October 1, 1968.

Like many others, it was not his choice to be in the Army. In Basic Training he sketched other men in his unit and his work was noticed at higher levels. Soon Jim was on his way to becoming a combat artist and after that, in the fall of 1969, he found himself in Vietnam, one of five artists assigned to Army Artist Team #9.

The Vietnam assignments for the artists were temporary, short-term and fast-paced, with the artists making quick sketches of the men and subjects they observed. Often they had only five or ten minutes to make these sketches in a combat zone. After approximately 60 days the artists were reassigned to Hawaii for 75 days to finish their work, turning sketches into paintings. The artists were given freedom to choose the subject of their paintings and were encouraged to use and develop their own unique styles. They worked independently and had the freedom to travel and spend time with different Army units all over Vietnam, from the Delta to the DMZ. All of the sketches and paintings, all of the creative work, became the property of the U.S. Army Art Collections, and would later be retained at the U.S. Army Center of Military History at Fort Belvoir, Virginia, 15 miles south of Washington D.C., where they are housed today.

In October 1969, Jim found himself near An Loc, with the 199th Light Infantry Brigade, about 60 miles northeast of Saigon. He spent about a week there, mostly with A and C Companies, 2nd Battalion, 3rd Regiment. His time was spent in the field with them, doing what they did, searching for "Charlie", the infamous Viet Cong. When he went on patrol with various units, he wasn't just a sketch artist/combat photographer, he also was an infantryman. His M.O.S. was 11B10 or 11 Bravo, rifleman. Along with cameras and a sketchbook, he carried an M-1 carbine and extra belts of ammo for the M60 machine gunner. He would sketch and take photos when time permitted, but there was also a war going on.

FIG 91- PFC. MARK MUEHE ON RIGHT

Near the end of the week he went on a night ambush patrol with one of the squads. The lieutenant who led the patrol simply said, "Stick close to us," before they moved out. As it was with Jim in all of these situations with different units, he was the new guy, an unknown factor and an unknown risk. The lieutenant wanted Jim nearby so he could keep an eye on him. Since the radio man was always close to the team leader, Jim was near Mark Muehe, who had the radio. The M60 machine gunner was also close, so Jim could quickly supply him with the additional belts of ammo he carried, if needed.

They didn't find any enemy on this ambush patrol and the night was uneventful. Jim had the opportunity to take a few photos of the men and made a few 5-minute sketches, but there was time for little else.

FIG 92 - JIM HARDY SKETCH OF MARK MUEHE

He stayed close to Mark, as ordered, but there was mostly silence, aside from brief whispers. They were out of radio contact while on this ambush patrol for fear of the VC monitoring the radio calls and at the end of the patrol, Jim learned that he was overdue on an assignment to another unit and that his commanding officer had been trying unsuccessfully to locate him for several days.

Later that day radio communication was restored, the squad was located and a LOH (Light Observation Helicopter) was sent to pick him up and take him to an assignment with the 82nd Airborne Division. Shortly thereafter, Mark's unit was ambushed and Mark was killed. Jim wasn't aware of

FIG 93 - JIM HARDY'S SKETCH OF LT. LITTLE

FIG 94 - LT. WILLIAM LITTLE SIGNING HIS SKETCH

Mark's death until much later. Many years later Jim learned that Lt. William Little, a platoon leader he served with on that same operation and whom he had sketched and photographed, had also been killed.[2]

After his 60-day assignment in Vietnam, Jim and the other artists were reassigned to Schofield Barracks on the island of Oahu to complete their artwork. He would spend three months there. Jim wanted to complete some etchings and they didn't have the necessary equipment (etching presses) at Schofield Barracks. The University of Hawaii in Honolulu did have what was needed and Jim got permission to use their equipment, so he decided to go there.

FIG 95 - MARK MUEHE STANDING ON LEFT WITH JIM HARDY ALONGSIDE HIM

There was no curfew and the artists had a lot of freedom. Jim took a Jeep to Honolulu and began using the equipment at the University. He met several students there, most of them hippies. Three of them (2 males and 1 female) shared an apartment. They told Jim he could sleep on their couch if he didn't want to drive back to the base every night. He took them up on their offer and spent a month, off and on, sleeping on their couch, occasionally reporting back to Schofield Barracks. There was no problem being off base as long as he kept in touch.

After the 90 days, he was sent back to Fort Ord, California, and reassigned to the laundry detail at his old training company. It was a safe, very boring assignment. As much as Jim hated the Vietnam War, he was restless and felt like he had deserted the guys back in Vietnam. He felt guilty that they were fighting the war and in danger while he was in a safe environment. They had to serve an entire year there, while he left after two months. It didn't seem right. With these things swirling in his mind, he volunteered to return to Vietnam.

On this tour he was assigned first to the 221st Signal Company for one month and then to the 1st Aviation Brigade, again as a combat artist/photographer for the remaining five months of his tour. During this tour he participated in the invasion of Cambodia as well as other combat operations. He returned home in September 1970 and was released from the Army just one day later.

Jim moved to Ocean Beach, California. He just wanted to unwind, to decompress, and to forget the war. He returned to what he loved most, surfing. He surfed, sketched and did woodcuts (from which he made prints) when he felt like it...and relaxed. During this time there was an important local criminal trial on TV, the trial of the San Diego mayor who was charged with bribery, and he had an idea, a possible way to make money, by sketching the courtroom activities. He contacted several of the local TV stations, but they weren't interested. He had another idea. He fabricated a fake Press

Pass, which got him into the courtroom without any problems. He began sketching the courtroom activities. People from the television news media saw him sketching, approached him, liked his sketches and purchased some of them. He had won after all and made some spending money.

In early 1971, Jim received a call from his former high school art teacher at Coronado High School and was offered a job teaching art. He accepted the temporary position and taught the remainder of the semester. Since he had G.I. Bill funds available, he decided to return to school and enrolled in the San Francisco Art Institute in the fall of that year to pursue a Master of Fine Arts Degree in print making. He obtained the degree but quickly realized that it was difficult to make a living as an artist. So he enrolled in a trade school to take a welding course, then got a job as a welder in the shipyards in San Francisco. He not only welded, but taught welding classes for several years to prospective welders. When the shipyards were closing and scaling back he realized the end was coming and became an inspector on the Golden Gate Bridge, inspecting welds.

While attending the San Francisco Art Institute, Jim was looking at copies of sketches he retained from Vietnam. He noted that he sketched an infantryman by the name of Albert Beltran, who was on that same ambush patrol with Mark Muehe and several others and saw from Albert's notation on the sketch that he lived in the San Francisco Bay Area at the time the sketch was made in Vietnam. He found Albert in the phone book and phoned him, only to learn that Mark Muehe was killed in an ambush on December 5, 1969. Jim didn't really know Mark, but sketched him and felt terrible about his death.

Later Jim learned of Lt. William Little's death from C Company, who, like Mark, was killed shortly after Jim left the unit. Others he sketched had been killed later in the war, but for some reason, Mark's death was particularly difficult for him to accept, perhaps because of the words Mark wrote beneath his name on the sketch, the words "I want to go home".

Time went on and Jim occasionally thought of Mark and the sketch. In the early 1980's Jim found Mark's father, Art Muehe, in the phone book, living in Bridgeview, Illinois, and called him. Jim explained that he served with Mark in Vietnam and had sketched him, as part of his job as a combat artist. He had also photographed Mark and some of his buddies and asked Art if he'd like a copy of the sketch and some of the photos. Art was happy to have these items and Jim mailed them to him.

A few years later Art and his wife visited Jim in California. Art didn't seem too interested in seeing all the sights, but did want to see the Golden Gate Bridge. Jim offered to take him there. It was while they were sitting on the sea wall, looking out across the Pacific Ocean that Art shared more about his son's death.

During the night on December 5, 1969, Art was asleep in bed and was awakened by something touching his toe. He awakened, looked through the darkness and saw Mark standing at the foot of his bed. Mark said, "I'm home Dad. Everything is okay. Don't worry." Then Mark disappeared. A day or two later when the Army notification team came to his door, Art thanked them and told them he knew why they were there…because Mark visited him that night and told him.

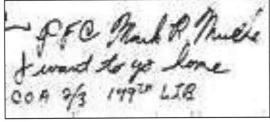

FIG 96 - MARK MUEHE'S WRITING ON SKETCH

Was Mark's visit that night real or was it just a dream? Art certainly thought it was real and the importance of those words Mark wrote on the sketch, "I want to go home," have haunted Jim since he first heard the story from Art Muehe. They still haunt him today. Were they simply the words of a young soldier longing for home and missing his family and friends…or was there more to it?

FIG 97 - JIM HARDY RECENTLY

Jim retired from his job as a seismic retrofit steel inspector on the Golden Gate Bridge in 2015. He and his wife, Melissa, have one son. They live in Martinez, California. Jim is a member of Viet Nam Veterans of Diablo Valley and is also a member of the Third Thursday Lunch Bunch, a group of Veterans who meet monthly in Concord, California.[3]

(See Appendix A for more of Jim Hardy's combat sketches.)

NOTES AND REFERENCES

[1] Both the Sorbonne and the Ecole des Beaux Arts are famous French universities. The Ecole des Beaux Arts has trained some of the most famous European artists during the past 350 years.

[2] 1st Lt. William F. Little III, of C Company, was killed by small arms fire on November 11, 1969.

[3] The author interviewed Jim Hardy for this story on September 15, 2016.

Chapter Twenty-One

A Valuable Classroom Lesson

Jim sat quietly in the Sociology class, feeling uncomfortable as the instructor announced that the topic for classroom discussion that day was the Vietnam War, from a social standpoint. The year was 1972 and he sat at one of the desks arranged in a circle with about 40 other students at the California College of Arts in Oakland, California. Jim, who had recently returned from Vietnam, soon realized that this wasn't going to be a good day.

Jim Murphy was a 22 year-old San Francisco native when this occurred. He grew up in nearby San Francisco, with a brother and two sisters and graduated from Mission High School. Jim was always interested in art. He even took summer classes in art while in high school. After graduating from high school in 1967, he enrolled at the Academy of Art in San Francisco. Unfortunately, he had only enough money to attend for one semester, so he had to drop out.

When Jim dropped out of school, he lost his college deferment and his status changed to 1A, making him eligible for the draft. He received his notice in the spring of 1968. Jim preferred to have some choice in his training, an unlikely option if he was drafted into the Army, so he went down to the Navy recruiting office and enlisted, with a 4-year commitment. He had hoped to increase his art skills in the Navy, but the Navy didn't have any openings for draftsmen, so he became an electrician's mate.

While still in the U.S. he received training to repair electrical systems on small boats. In the summer of 1969, while still in training, he married his wife Pat. In November 1969, Jim was on his way overseas, to Sasebo Naval Base in Japan, where he was assigned to the repair ship USS Ajax. Sasebo was the home port for the ship, but while there the Ajax was deployed on 1-month long assignments to Vietnam, to the coastal city of Vung Tau. While there he repaired smaller boats, like the river patrol boats (PBRs), Swift boats (PFFs), Mike boats (LCMs), and LSTs. All of these smaller boats were capable of navigating the numerous rivers and waterways of Vietnam. After his first tour ended he returned to San Diego, but was redeployed to Sasebo and spent more time on temporary assignments at Vung Tau.

FIG 98 - PETTY OFFICER 3RD CLASS JIM MURPHY

Jim's enlistment commitment ended in July 1972. By then he and his wife had one daughter and would soon have another. One evening soon after he left the Navy, he and his wife had some of their high school friends over for dinner. Most of the guests were friends who had attended San Francisco State College with Pat. During the evening some of their friends began talking about Vietnam and were critical of America's role there. Jim entered into the discussion, feeling he had to defend the U.S. involvement in Vietnam. The comments that followed clearly indicated the others didn't share his opinion. He didn't feel good about the discussion and made a conscious decision to avoid the topic in the future whenever possible.

Jim's goal was to complete his education and go into graphic design. The G.I. Bill was available, so with his wife's support he applied and was accepted at the California College of Arts. He worked part-time for the first six months and his wife also worked. He later received some scholarships, which allowed him to quit his part-time job and commit totally to finishing his education.

There were two other Vets in Jim's class that day in 1972. He didn't know them, but knew they were Vets because he had seen them in the office where he stopped by on a monthly basis to sign for and receive the G.I. Bill benefit check. He could see the uncomfortable looks on their faces as the young professor began to voice his anti-Vietnam feelings to the class.

Soon the students began to voice their own sentiments about the Vietnam War, encouraged by the instructor. All of the comments were anti-Vietnam and many were anti-Vet. The professor encouraged the students to continue to share their views, as the discussion became louder and more intense, with the professor feeding the frenzy. A primary focus turned to those who actually served in Vietnam. The term "baby killers" was used repeatedly. One student commented that anyone who served was naive or just plain stupid. Another said that those who served should be treated as war criminals. Similar comments followed. It was almost frightening to see this kind of rage and anger, particularly when it was encouraged by the professor. Jim and the other Vets just sat quietly. Fortunately, the other students didn't know there were Vets in the class.[1]

The class ended after 45 minutes. As the three Vets began to leave, one suggested they go and have coffee, so they did. One asked, "What the Hell just happened?" They discussed it while they sat there, but there were no clear answers. They were still confused when they finished their coffee and went their separate ways that day.

This classroom incident strengthened Jim's resolve to avoid talking about Vietnam at all costs and to not tell people he was a Vietnam Vet. There was no point in making himself so vulnerable or subject himself to this kind of criticism, so he tried to move on. He finished college in 2 1/2 years with a Bachelor of Fine Arts degree (BFA) in Graphic Design.

Jim went on to have a 40+ year career in Marketing and Design, working for major companies like Hewlitt Packard, Visa, Carnation, Wells Fargo, Del Monte, Clorox, Fetzer and Robert Mondavi Wineries. After the bad experience in college, he just avoided any discussions about Vietnam or telling anyone that he was a Vietnam Vet. He didn't expect that people would respect him for his service to his country, but it also became increasingly clear that his service wasn't even accepted by many.

In the mid-1990's, some of the men he worked with were having a conversation. The topic turned to the Vietnam years and the guys were telling stories about how they avoided the draft and military service during those years. Jim said nothing, but listened as the others talked about their own individual experiences. One of the executives noticed that Jim wasn't saying anything and in an effort to include him in the conversation, asked how he managed to avoid serving. Jim answered simply, "I didn't." The man, who also happened to be the vice president of the company, asked, "Did you serve in Vietnam?" Jim answered, "Yes". Jim could tell the men were surprised. It was an awkward situation and the conversation ended. Three of those involved in that conversation later apologized. Times had changed and although it's unlikely the apologies would have been offered 15 years earlier, it was still an uncomfortable topic.

Jim heard about the Viet Nam Veterans of Diablo Valley in the early 1990's. His friend and fellow Vietnam Vet Bill Green told him about the group and he attended a meeting. He didn't feel vulnerable when he was with these Vets. He didn't sit around with them and discuss Vietnam on a regular basis, but he knew

FIG 99 - JIM MURPHY TODAY

they weren't going to attack him for serving his country and he felt comfortable in this setting with those who had also served and understood. He joined the group.

In 2014, Jim retired. At that time he was the Director of Creative Services Globally for Jelly Belly Candy Company. Always interested in art, he now spends time painting. He and Pat have two daughters and three grandchildren and live in Danville, California.

The specific details of Jim's story may be unique, but the general theme is similar to what many of the Vets experienced after their return to civilian life, particularly so in the San Francisco Bay Area. The Vets who spent careers in the military generally had it a little easier because they were surrounded by other Veterans, but there was still the stigma of being a Vietnam Vet.

When the Vets returned from Vietnam some could understand the protests against the war. What made it even more difficult was that many of the protesters didn't stop there, but also felt the need to attack their fellow Americans who were called into the war. It was, and continues to be, a difficult pill for many Vets to swallow.

The Vietnam War impacted the Vets in various ways, but the vast majority, like Jim Murphy, went on to lead successful lives. This is in spite of the fact that some had serious and permanent physical injuries, while others suffered from and continue to suffer from PTSD. Others have illnesses directly related to Agent Orange, a defoliant used extensively in Vietnam. Several forms of cancer have been directly attributed to the exposure to Agent Orange.

The effects of Vietnam haven't ended with the Vets. In many cases their experiences impacted their families as well. (See Appendix B for a son's story about growing up with a father who is a Vietnam Vet.) In other cases, there have been physical impacts on families. Bill LaVigne, (see *I Didn't Even*

Know His Name chapter) was one of many combat Vets exposed to Agent Orange during his tour. Bill's son, Hooper, was born with severe spina bifida, which has been attributed to Bill's exposure to Agent Orange. The V.A. accepted responsibility for this condition and is taking care of the medical costs, but Bill's son and others like him are as much the casualties of the war as those who experienced it firsthand.[2]

NOTES AND REFERENCES

[1] The term "baby killer" was commonly used in anti-Vietnam protests after the media released information on what has been commonly referred to as the "My Lai Massacre". The incident occurred on March 16, 1968, when an infantry platoon led by Lt. William Calley was accused of murdering several hundred Vietnamese civilians. More than a year later the news media became aware of the story and several stories were published, along with TV coverage. The term "baby killer" had been used previously in reference to Vietnam, but became a more commonplace term after information on Lt. Calley and his men was released. Calley was later convicted of murdering Vietnamese civilians. It is the author's opinion, based on conversations with former students, police officers and others who witnessed large anti-Vietnam protests in California, along with events he personally witnessed and news footage and photos from the time period, that it would have been a rarity in California for a large demonstration or protest to have occurred without a placard or poster referencing American servicemen in Vietnam as being "baby killers", protesting both the war and the warriors. (See chapter 15 for additional reference to this theme.)

[2] Jim Murphy was interviewed for this story on 3/31/17.

Chapter Twenty-Two

As Saigon Fell

Dave Smith wasn't in Saigon when it fell to Communist forces on April 30, 1975, but he had a front seat to some of the rippling effects of those last days. It happened during his second tour to Southeast Asia as an Air Force navigator.

Dave was an Air Force brat. His dad was an Air Force pilot and he and his two siblings moved around a lot with the family, living in Colorado, France and Japan before moving to California. After high school he attended Long Beach State College in California. While there he enrolled in Air Force R.O.T.C. and received his commission when he graduated in 1970, while the Vietnam War was still going strong. He subsequently attended navigation school and became a navigator.

Dave was eventually assigned as a navigator in the 42nd Tactical Electronic Warfare Squadron, 388th Tactical Fighter Wing. His plane was the EB-66. It was a twin-engine jet aircraft, originally designed to be a light bomber in the mid-1950's when it first entered production. By the time the

Vietnam War came around, its role had changed and it was converted into an electronic warfare aircraft. It no longer carried bombs, but was now equipped with highly sophisticated equipment to jam the radar-guided SAMs (Surface-to-Air Missiles) that were taking their toll against American fighters and bombers in the skies over North Vietnam.

There were two configurations of the EB-66 that Dave would be flying. The planes were used for two different roles, to jam enemy radar sites and for reconnaissance. The EB-66E carried three crewmen, a pilot, a navigator and an electronic warfare officer or EWO. In this configuration Dave's position as navigator was behind the pilot. The EWO sat across from him with his jamming equipment. This was the plane they used to jam radar sites over North Vietnam and along the passes leading to the Ho Chi Minh trail, in order to protect the fighter bombers and B-52s on their bombing missions.

FIG 100 - DAVE SMITH WITH B-66 IN BACKGROUND

Dave also flew in the EB-66C. Dave's position was the same in the aircraft, with an observer sitting across from him. This plane had a 7-man crew, with four electronic warfare officers and their equipment in the bomb bay of the plane. This plane was used for reconnaissance.

Upon his arrival at a base in Korat, Thailand, Dave began flying combat missions in January 1973, during a time of uncertainty. Korat was a Royal Thai Air Force base, but was also the home of the U.S. Air Force 388th Tactical Fighter wing. The month before, in December, there had been extensive bombings of North Vietnam, code-named Linebacker II.

Peace negotiations had been ongoing in Paris for several years, but the war continued. In early December 1972, President Nixon issued an ultimatum to the North Vietnamese, demanding they return to the peace discussions within 72 hours. There was no response, so Nixon ordered massive, intense bombings of mainly the Hanoi and Haiphong areas, which began on December 18th. The intent of these raids was to bring the North Vietnamese back to the negotiating table and end the war. After several days of bombings, on December 25th, the North Vietnamese agreed to more negotiations and these intense bombings ended on December 29th. Peace negotiations were re-established several days later, but there were still some combat missions over North Vietnam, but nothing north of the 20th parallel.[1]

The missions over the north were completely suspended on January 15th, when President Nixon announced the end of all offensive actions against the north. A peace treaty was signed on January 27th. With this agreement, the U.S. agreed to halt all military activities in Vietnam and to withdraw our troops within 60 days. In return, the North Vietnamese agreed to an immediate ceasefire and agreed to release all of the American POWs within 60 days.

Dave flew several combat missions early in January, before the combat missions were suspended and the treaty was signed. On the jamming missions they accompanied F-105 fighter bombers to the target and jammed the missile sites around the target with their specialized equipment while the fighters attacked. In addition, they flew reconnaissance missions.

He downplays his role in the raids, and is quick to point out that, although there was danger from anti-aircraft fire and missiles should the missiles get through, it couldn't be compared to what the infantry experienced on the ground. Dave lived in relative comfort and decent living conditions. He could go to the bar and have a drink or a cold beer when he wasn't flying.

After mid-January, Dave's unit didn't fly over North Vietnam and their role shifted more to reconnaissance. They were prohibited from flying within one mile of the North Vietnamese border. The missions were now over Laos, Cambodia and South Vietnam only. Soon the air division restricted flights to within two miles of the border and then orders came down from his wing restricting flights to within three miles of the border. The powers-that-be wanted no border incidents to interfere with the truce.

As navigator, one of Dave's roles was to make certain that his aircraft didn't stray over the border and create an international incident. He flew his last jamming mission on April 16th, accompanying four separate flights of B-52s on a bombing mission over the Plain of Jars in Laos, providing electronic counter measures (jamming) in support of Royal

Laotian forces fighting Communist-backed Pathet Lao troops. Although the Americans were leaving, the war was far from over in the region as North Vietnam continued its war against South Vietnam and in Laos. After this, Dave continued flying reconnaissance missions until his tour ended in December and he returned home.[2]

Dave stayed in the Air Force after he returned. He met his girlfriend, a naval officer, whom he would later marry. He remained a navigator, but transitioned to KC-135s, an aerial tanker version of the famous Boeing 707. In 1975, he found himself assigned to an air refueling squadron at Robins Air Force Base in Georgia. He and his unit were deployed on an 8-week temporary duty assignment to Thailand and Guam. For the first six weeks he was stationed at U-Tapao Royal Thai Navy Airfield. This is where he found himself in April.

Since Dave's last deployment, the North Vietnamese had continued their offensive into South Vietnam and the Communist Pathet Lao now controlled most of Laos. Most of Cambodia had also been taken over by Communist troops. By April 1975, the North Vietnamese controlled most of South Vietnam, while Communist troops had done the same in Cambodia and Laos and North Vietnamese troops were approaching Saigon.

Near the base at U-Tapao, Dave saw that refugee camps were being constructed along the beach with hundreds of evacuees from Cambodia already being housed there. They were on alert several times in early April, with various scenarios surfacing, all having to do with the Communist takeover of Laos and Cambodia and the looming evacuation of Saigon as Communist troops approached. Several thousand Americans and pro-American Vietnamese remained in Saigon and the danger increased for them every day as Communist troops neared Saigon. On the 12th of April, the U.S. ambassador to Cambodia, John Dean, arrived at U-Tapao, having been evacuated from Phnom Penh in a U.S. Marine helicopter. Cambodia had all but fallen. More Cambodian refugees arrived by helicopter the following day.

Without U.S. support it seemed that all of Southeast Asia, with the exception of Thailand, would soon be under Communist control. Among other aircraft, approximately 20 B-52s were stationed at U-Tapao. Dave's squadron was there to refuel the big planes and other American aircraft. Tensions mounted as the end of the month approached. It was clear that Saigon would soon fall to the Communists. South Vietnamese planes began flying in, seeking refuge and safety. After landing, they were parked on one of the ramps.

By April 29th, the situation in Saigon was critical. Communist troops were on the edge of Saigon. U-Tapao, 350 miles from Saigon, was becoming a safe haven for Vietnamese who could get there by plane. That morning Dave was sitting on the runway in his aircraft, waiting to take off. Their role would be to refuel American planes, should their assistance be needed. The U.S. still maintained a presence in the region and American F-4 Phantoms and A-7 Corsair fighters still patrolled the skies. His plane was 4th in line, getting ready to turn onto the active runway, when an emergency call came in over the radio. A South Vietnamese C-119 transport plane was 22 miles out, incoming and declared an emergency, requesting immediate clearance to land. The four refueling planes needed to take-off ASAP to get off the runway.

Their 60-second take-off interval was now changed to 15 seconds. The first and second planes quickly took off, but the plane in front of Dave's plane aborted on the runway, with a mechanical problem. Dave's pilot waited while that aircraft taxied off the runway. Now it was their turn as they lined up for the take off. Then they themselves had a mechanical problem. As the C-119 approached they were able to get off the runway and on to a taxi way. Their plane was repaired within 30 minutes, so they taxied out again.

With all of the action and more than 30 aircraft in front of them waiting to take off, they never did make it off the ground, but sat in their "metal box" of an airplane for more than 6 hours in 97-degree heat. While sitting there they saw an amazing site.

The Vietnamese continued to land in all kinds of aircraft, cargo C-119s, C-130s, C-47ss and C-7s along with single seat F-5 jet fighters, A-37s and A-1 propeller-driven attack aircraft. On this day they all became cargo aircraft and their cargo was pro-American Vietnamese, both civilian and military, desperately fleeing Vietnam. All were packed with people. One C-130, which could normally carry fewer than 100 people, had 240. One of the A-1s, which normally carried two men, had 12 people aboard. One F-5 fighter had the pilot, his wife and two children. One of the C-47s blew a tire and crash-landed on the runway, closing it temporarily until it could be towed off. The C-47, which could carry 30 troops, had more than 100 Vietnamese onboard. Landings continued all day long, one after another, with planes landing on both ends of the runway, some without clearance.[3]

U-Tapao wasn't the only destination for these planes. Carriers off the coast were also receiving refugees on helicopters and planes and others had flown into Clark Air Force Base in the Philippines. The Vietnamese who had assisted the Americans throughout the war were fearful of revenge and retaliation and many of those who had the ability to flee did so, military as well as civilians and their families.

The next day, April 30th, it was over. No more aircraft were coming from Saigon. Airfields had been overrun. Dave made it over to the U.S. Navy ramp, where a large contingent of Vietnamese planes were parked, surrounded by security guards. Dave wanted to get a photo of all the Vietnamese planes, but security police wouldn't let him anywhere near the planes and they weren't allowed to take photos.

On May 1st, Dave was able to get a closer look at the field full of Vietnamese planes. The Vietnamese markings were being painted out. Thailand was in a difficult position, trying to maintain its neutrality in the region. There was no question that the North Vietnamese wanted to take possession of these planes for their own Air Force. One possible way to avoid this was to show that they weren't Vietnamese and the Thais were making every effort to do so.

A day or so later Dave sat at the bar at The Green Latrine, the local watering hole. As he sat there drinking Singha beer with his pilot and copilot he saw an unusual sight. U.S. Air Force helicopters had some of the F-5 fighters suspended beneath them in slings, taking them out to the gulf. He later learned that the USS Midway, a carrier, was sitting offshore and this was the destination of the Vietnamese aircraft. They were trying to put them into U.S. hands before the North Vietnamese claimed them and demanded their return. Dave watched as one of the helicopters started to sway. Clearly in danger of losing control, it dropped its F-5 cargo into the water and recovered. This was still better than turning the fighter over to the North Vietnamese. He watched as more planes were carried offshore by the lumbering helicopters.

FIG 101 - HELICOPTER WITH F5 ON SLING (U-TAPAO)

During the second week of May Dave's squadron left Thailand and flew to Anderson Air Force base on Guam. He was surprised to see several thousand refugees at temporary camps there, likely some of the same refugees he had seen in Thailand. One would have thought it would be a more relaxing time, since Saigon had already fallen, but there was another crisis.

On May 12th, Communist Khmer troops from Cambodia seized an American container ship, the SS Mayaguez and its crew that they claimed was in their waters. Once again, the American crews in Guam were put on alert. Although U.S. planes still based in Thailand were much closer to respond, Thailand's neutrality was a very delicate matter, and it would be difficult for American planes there to get involved. If B-52 bombers were needed, they would come from Guam, refueled by Dave and his buddies in their KC-135s. It was a tense situation and war could easily break out again.

On May 15th, a briefing was held at 2:00AM. The B-52s were being loaded with bombs and the KC-135s would be refueling them. At 4:30AM Dave was sitting in his aircraft, waiting for the pilot to start the engines, when the mission was called off and the crews went back inside. They were told that 10:00 would now be the earliest take-off time. The mission was later cancelled. Dave later learned the crew of the Mayaguez was released and the ship was recovered, but not before several American lives were lost.[4]

So this was how Dave's war ended. He flew home several days later. He stayed in the Air Force, retiring as a Lt. Colonel in 1993. There were many more assignments, including a stint as a navigator in the Presidential Support Unit. Dave never set foot in Vietnam, yet he participated in some of the final combat missions over Vietnam, had a ringside seat to see some of the results of the mass evacuation as Saigon fell and was sitting in an aircraft, waiting to take-off, as the U.S. nearly entered another conflict in Southeast Asia.

He has been married to his wife Jan for 40 years and they have two adult sons. After he retired, Dave worked as a wireless logistics manager for several years, retiring again in 2005. He also coached wrestling for 14 years at California High School, in San Ramon, retiring in 2014.

Dave and Jan live in San Ramon, California. As well as being an active member of Viet Nam Veterans of Diablo Valley, Dave belongs to MOAA (Military Officers Association of America) and volunteers for Loaves & Fishes, an organization that provides meals to those in need.[5]

FIG 102 - DAVE SMITH TODAY

NOTES AND REFERENCES

[1] These missions were also known as "The Christmas bombings" for obvious reasons.

[2] On February 22, 1973, Prince Souvanna signed a cease-fire with the Pathet Lao. Despite this, fighting continued between the Pathet Lao and royalist troops around the town of Paksong. Souvanna requested assistance for his troops from the U.S. and several strikes were made in the area in late February. Souvanna again requested assistance in April and the U.S. provided assistance in the form of B-52 raids on April 16th and April 17th. These were the final bombing missions.

[3] Dave's recollections of these events are contained in a letter he wrote to his girlfriend, Jan, and some of the information is also from Escape to U-Taphao, Air & Space Magazine, January 1997.

[4] USAF helicopters carried Marines to Koh Tang Island in the Gulf of Thailand, where the crew of the SS Mayaguez was thought to be held. They invaded the island and a pitched battle ensued, with several losses of Marines and Air Force personnel from the helicopters. The crew was not on the island, but was subsequently released. Marines aboard the destroyer USS Holt boarded the ship, which was unoccupied and returned it to U.S. custody.

[5] Dave Smith was interviewed for this story on 11/30/16.

Chapter Twenty-Three

The Vietnam Years

Much has been said and written about the unrest occurring during the Vietnam War. Nowhere were the signs of unrest more visible than in the San Francisco Bay Area. U.C. Berkeley was a hotbed of protests and it would seem that historically liberal San Francisco had become a haven for those who didn't fit elsewhere, including anarchists and those from other radical groups.

The returning Vets wanted peace and quiet. They didn't get it. Military ships that entered the Bay Area beneath the Golden Bridge were often met with objects being tossed at them from the bridge as they looked up at protest signs on the bridge. Those flying into the San Francisco International Airport were met with protests and harsh words. Those who flew into nearby Travis Air Force Base on their return took off their uniforms on arrival and donned civilian attire for the bus ride to the Bay Area. It simply wasn't safe or prudent to be off-base in uniform.[1]

Protests at U.C. Berkeley had been occurring since the early 60's, many of them related to what was called the "free speech" movement in the early days. As the Vietnam War escalated, this became a primary focus at U.C. Berkeley. The anti-war element gained momentum, fueled by the near proximity of several military bases, including the Oakland Army Terminal, Treasure Island Naval Base, Alameda Naval Air Station, and 6th Army Headquarters at the Presidio, San Francisco. It was a recipe for disaster. By 1967, the protests grew violent.

Other radical groups also gained momentum during this same time. The unrest wasn't solely related to the Vietnam War. The Black Panther Party, a radical black group spewing hatred, was figuring prominently in local news, often with acts of violence. In 1969, a radical American Indian group took over Alcatraz Island.

Students for a Democratic Society (SDS) had gained a foothold at U.C. Berkeley. It was one of the groups involved in the free speech movement. By 1966, they had taken up the slogan "From Protest To Resistance" and the group was very active in the various protests at U.C. Berkeley.

One of the contenders for the most violent radical group was the Weather Underground. Originally a faction of SDS, this organization advocated revolution and the overthrow of the U.S. government by violence, claiming responsibility for several of the bombings in the Bay Area.[2]

These were angry times and this was what returning Vietnam War Vets faced on their return. For those who returned after 1967, it was worse.

It didn't help matters that the returning Vets looked different. While most college students had longer hair, the returning Vets who chose to enroll in college were immediately noticeable with their short military haircuts. They couldn't blend in, even if they wanted to, at least not until their hair grew out. Some of them just dropped out.[3]

Following is a summary of some of the larger events that were occurring in the Bay Area during these troubled times.[4]

- May 22, 1965-Members of Young Socialist Alliance march on the Berkeley Draft Board where they hang Lyndon Johnson in effigy and burn draft cards.
- August 15, 1965-Thousands of protestors march on the Oakland Army induction center.
- November 20, 1965-Members of the Vietnam Day Committee (VDC) stage a protest at DeFremery Park in Oakland.
- April 20, 1966-A bomb explodes in the Vietnam Day Committee office in Berkeley. Committee members stage a demonstration on Telegraph Avenue in Berkeley, which is forcibly broken up by the police.
- October 15, 1966-The radical Black Panther Party is formed in Oakland, California.
- September 27, 1966-Hunter's Point riot occurs in San Francisco. A 3-day race riot breaks out when a white police officer shoots and kills a black suspect. The National Guard is called in to assist San Francisco PD in restoring order.
- November 30, 1966-There is a sit-down protest at the Navy recruiting table in the U.C. Berkeley Student Union.
- January 1, 1967-The Black Panther Party officially opens up its headquarters in Oakland.
- April 15, 1967-In San Francisco, thousands march to Golden Gate Park in protest of the Vietnam War.

- October 16, 1967-During "Stop the Draft" week thousands march to the Oakland Army Induction Center, handing out leaflets and refusing to disperse.
- On October 17, 1967-4,000 protesters attempted to keep inductees from reporting at the Oakland Army Induction Center. Arrests that week include folksinger Joan Baez.
- October 28, 1967-Oakland Police Officer John Frey is killed and Officer Herbert Haines is wounded by two members of the Black Panther Party, Huey Newton and Gene McKinney.
- December 4, 1967-Hundreds gather at the Federal Building in San Francisco to protest the Draft. Draft cards are burned as part of the event.
- January 8, 1968-A large group gathers at the Fairmont Hotel in San Francisco to protest a speech by Secretary of State Dean Rusk. The gathering turns violent and there are several arrests.
- May 17, 1968-800+ students at U.C. Berkeley hold a separate, unauthorized graduation event, signing a petition affirming they will not serve in the U.S. military.
- April 6, 1968-Black Panthers ambush Oakland Police Officers. Black Panther Eldridge Cleaver is wounded. Another Black Panther, Bobby Hutton, dies in the shootout. Several other Panthers are arrested.
- June 30, 1968-The Berkeley mayor declares a state of emergency in Berkeley due to rioting and enacts a 3-day curfew in the wake of earlier violent protests.
- October 14, 1968-The Presidio Mutiny occurs at the Presidio Stockade, part of the U.S. Army facility in San Francisco, three days after an unarmed prisoner was shot and killed by a guard. 27 prisoners staged a sit-in

and were subsequently tried for mutiny under the Code of Military Justice. The protest was allegedly over prison conditions, combined with anti-war sentiments.[5]

- October 23, 1968-U.C. Berkeley students barricade themselves in Moses Hall on campus to protest the Regents' refusal to allow Black Panther Eldridge Cleaver to teach an accredited class.

- November 6, 1968-San Francisco State University students go on strike accusing the school of racial discrimination. The event shuts down the campus and police are called in by University President S.I. Hayakawa.

- January 4, 1969-San Francisco State President Hayakawa bans speeches, rallies, marches and other disruptive events on campus.

- February 5, 1969-Governor Ronald Reagan declares "a state of extreme emergency" on the U.C. Berkeley campus and authorizes the California Highway Patrol to move in and assist the Alameda County Sheriff's office. This is in response to ongoing clashes between the police and protestors during the past several days.

- March 22, 1969-Mills College students in Oakland California, with Black Students Union members, seize college president Robert Werk's office, holding him hostage and make demands for more minority involvement in student affairs.

- April 5, 1969-On the anniversary of Martin Luther King's death, protestors fight with police at the Presidio.

- May 15, 1969-People's Park riots take place at U.C. Berkeley. When police attempt to take back a piece of public land on the U.C. Berkeley campus, several hundred protestors attack the police. According to reports at the time more than 100 police officers are injured. More than 50 protestors are treated for gunshot pellet wounds and one student, James Rector, dies from a gunshot wound. Governor Ronald Reagan calls in the National Guard to restore order and the National Guard remained on scene for 17 days.[6]

- May 19, 1967-U.C. Berkeley professors hold a vigil to protest the police handling of the People's Park riot.
- November 20, 1969-Radical American Indians occupy Alcatraz Island, calling themselves Indians of All Tribes (IAT), claiming the island is theirs under the 1868 Treaty of Laramie. They occupy the island until June 1971, when they are forced off by government employees.
- February 13, 1970-Bombs explode outside the Berkeley Police station, injuring officers.
- February 16, 1970-A bomb explodes at a San Francisco Police sub-station (Park Station), killing Officer Brian McDonnell and wounding Officer Frank Rath. [7]
- April 15, 1970-Students attack the U.S. Navy ROTC building at U.C. Berkeley.
- May 1, 1970-Massive riots take place on the U.C. Berkeley campus, lasting several days, protesting the U.S. invasion of Cambodia.
- July 27, 1970-Bombs explode at the Presidio in San Francisco.
- August 19, 1970-A rally at the Civic Center in San Francisco in support of Black Panther Angela Davis ends in a clash between demonstrators and the police.
- August 20, 1970-Berkeley Police Officer Ronald Tsukamoto is murdered on a traffic stop by an unknown black male. No one is ever prosecuted, but

rumors surfaced that members of one of the radical local groups killed him.

- October 7, 1970-A bomb explodes outside the Marin Courthouse.
- October 22, 1970-A bomb explodes outside Brendan Church in San Francisco at the funeral of San Francisco Police Officer Harold Hamilton, who was murdered three days prior. Black Liberation Army members are arrested for the bombing years later.
- February 4, 1971-A bomb explodes in front of the Oakland Induction Center in the early morning hours.
- March 30, 1971-A bomb is discovered on the roof of Mission Police Station in San Francisco. Members of the Black Liberation Army are later arrested and charged.
- April 24, 1971-There is an anti-war protest rally in San Francisco. One estimate indicates 150,000 attended.
- August 29, 1971-San Francisco Police Sergeant John Young is murdered at Ingleside Police Station in San Francisco when two men armed with shotguns enter and shoot him several times. Members of the Black Liberation Army were charged with the murder in 2007.
- August 29, 1971-The Office of California Prisons in San Francisco is bombed.

The violence didn't occur just in the cities, but also filtered out into the suburbs in the San Francisco Bay Area. One such incident occurred in the quiet town of San Rafael, at the Marin County courthouse. On August 7, 1970, George Jackson, an inmate at Soledad Prison and a Black Panther, was being tried for the murder of John Mills, a Soledad Prison guard. James McClain, another Black Panther, was being tried for stabbing a Soledad Prison guard. Jonathan Jackson, George's brother, managed to smuggle three firearms into the courtroom. The guns had been purchased by Angela Davis, Black Panther activist and former UCLA professor.

Judge Harold Haley was taken hostage, along with four others including three jurors and Deputy D.A. Gary Thomas. Jonathan Jackson and three accomplices took the five hostages out onto the street, put them into a truck and began to drive. Before leaving, the hostage takers demanded the release of George Jackson and two others being tried with him. As the vehicle drove off police returned fire after McClain shot at them. A short distance away the police had set up a road block. In the ensuing gun battle Judge Haley was killed when a shotgun taped to his neck went off. Three of the Black Panther hostage-takers were shot and killed and only one survived. Deputy D.A. Thomas was shot and paralyzed and one juror was slightly wounded.

Across the San Francisco Bay in sleepy Walnut Creek, another violent incident occurred months later. On a weekend night the Boy Scouts held a regional event in the Las Lomas High School gymnasium, an event to honor American Indians. The Walnut Creek Police received a call about some American Indians creating a disturbance at the event.

Officer Ron O'Dell responded to the high school. He walked through the hall to the gymnasium, where he found a group of 20-30 American Indians in front of the entrance. A woman collecting tickets at a booth by the door was obviously frightened and asked O'Dell to help her. At this point the Indians were trying to force their way into the gymnasium. O'Dell pushed past them and went through the doorway, pulling the doors shut behind him in an effort to keep the intruders outside. His efforts failed and he was attacked and knocked to the gym floor. They started kicking him and hitting him and tried to get his gun out of its holster. O'Dell managed to hold onto the gun, but his night stick was taken from him, along with his portable radio and thrown across the floor. O'Dell held onto his gun for dear life as the beating continued, ultimately resulting in a broken nose and other injuries. He was finally able to crawl across the floor, retrieve his radio and call for help.

The first arriving officer was Doug Silva, who rode through the hall on his police motorcycle. As Silva got off his motorcycle, one of the Indians rushed him, swinging the baton that had been taken from O'Dell. The first blow, aimed at Silva's head, shattered Silva's motorcycle helmet. Silva drew his weapon, but didn't fire. Several other officers arrived, but could not gain control of the crowd. Ultimately several other police agencies were called in to quell the disturbance. Several of the Indians were subsequently arrested. This group was associated with the group that occupied Alcatraz at the time.[8]

Neither of the aforementioned incidents was directly associated with the Vietnam War, but both demonstrate the unrest, violence and tension at the time in the San Francisco Bay Area. Other protests were occurring elsewhere, although not as regularly and generally in not as large a scale.

U.C. Davis is just 100 miles from San Francisco, and even in this more conservative atmosphere, protests occurred, with groups like SDS and the group "Resistance" spearheading the efforts. Unlike Berkeley, in Davis the protests were more peaceful, although almost daily anti-war articles appeared in *The California Aggie*, the U.C. Davis newspaper, often describing the more violent events that occurred in nearby Berkeley. An April 1970 story referenced the occupation of the Navy R.O.T.C. building on campus by 150 students. Unlike similar incidents at U.C. Berkeley, there was no reported violence and the "occupation" lasted only 7 ½ hours.[9]

Across the nation, Kent State University in Ohio had one of the most notable protests that turned to violence on May 4, 1970. At the end of April, President Nixon announced that U.S. troops had entered Cambodia. On May 1st, several hundred students held an anti-war protest. Late that evening people leaving a bar began throwing bottles at police cars. The situation escalated and the entire police force was called in to deal with the situation. The next day there was a large demonstration on campus and the ROTC building was set afire. The Mayor had already asked for assistance from the Ohio Army National Guard.

On May 4th, a large scheduled protest began at noon. The police had given a dispersal order, but the students ignored it. Tear gas was dispensed by the National Guard, but it was ineffective and the students stayed. The situation worsened and the National Guard troops opened fire, killing four students and wounding nine others.

One of the most famous or infamous radicals of the time was actress Jane Fonda. She gained notoriety for her 1972 trip to Hanoi, North Vietnam. She's remembered most for a photo of her sitting on an anti-aircraft gun in Hanoi. She also met with several American POWs in Hanoi, later describing the good and humane treatment they were receiving. About their treatment she commented, "They were in such good physical and medical shape." The truth was revealed when the POWs were released in the spring of 1974 and the truth was revealed about the torture and deprivation they received.[10]

Fonda is lesser known for her radio broadcasts from North Vietnam to American troops, telling the troops they were committing murder. Her behavior was demoralizing to many American troops and some wanted her tried as a war criminal. She and anti-war activist/actor Donald Sutherland also went on a tour they called the "FTA" Tour, an anti-war road show, visiting military towns along the West Coast, broadcasting and trying to gain support for their anti-war message.[11]

Meanwhile, the draft was in full force. Able-bodied young men who didn't want to be drafted in California did have a temporary advantage that wasn't available in some states. California had junior colleges (now called community colleges). In the 1960's and early 1970's nearly everyone was able to attend these 2-year colleges, since there was no tuition. Even if they didn't continue on to a 4-year institution, as long as they carried what was considered a "full load" or 15 semester units or credits and maintained a 2.0 grade point average (C) they could avoid the draft for two years. After that, if they were able-bodied and in good health, their draft status changed to 1A, making them eligible for the draft.

In 1969 the rules changed for the draft and much of the power was taken away from the local draft boards to determine who would be drafted. A lottery system was instituted nationally for draft-eligible males. The first lottery was held on December 1, 1969, for males born between January 1, 1944 and December 31, 1950. Three subsequent yearly lotteries were held, the last being in 1972, for those born in 1953. None were called up from this lottery, since the draft was abolished in 1973.

The way this worked is a number was drawn for each day of the year. For instance the number drawn for July 27th was 289. What this meant was that if the necessary number of men was called up for the year 1970 had reached its quota, the person with number 289 would not be drafted. If the quota hadn't been reached the individual would be drafted. Unlike the previous system the individual was only subject to the draft for one year, not until he reached a certain age. Students with college deferments could decide whether they wanted to keep their deferment until they finished college or take their chances in the draft for that year.

The draft was a regular conversation topic among young adults, since the draft had a potential impact on so many. When asked, "What's your number?" in those days, it had an entirely different meaning than today. It was often someone inquiring about a young man's draft number, not a request for a phone number. It was clearly a different time.

This is the environment to which the Vietnam Vets returned in the San Francisco Bay area. They would not find peace here.

NOTES AND REFERENCES

[1] Things weren't as bad for the returning Vets prior to 1968, but from that time on the returning Vets were often told not to wear their uniforms.

[2] More recent stories about these groups have shed a different light into some of them, even showing them as humanitarian organizations, but one only has to read documents produced by the groups themselves to learn their true

nature. *Prairie Fire*, listing Bill Ayers and others as the authors in the Weather Underground, clearly shows the group's motives, even acknowledging specific bombings. *The Black Panther Party Manifesto* outlines the beliefs of that group.

[3] One of those who dropped out as a result of this was Bill Green. See chapter "A Decent Proposal".

[4] There were almost daily protests that weren't as noteworthy, because of their smaller size or because they were overshadowed by larger events (particularly in Berkeley).

[5] At least most of the sentences were later reduced to "Willful disobedience of a superior officer".

[6] Source: University of California Police Dept. website and 3/21/17 interview with former Berkeley PD police officer Bob Tietjen. A plot of land purchased by U.C. Berkeley with the original purpose of building student housing on it. As it sat vacant in the planning stages, it was taken over and occupied by students and others, declaring it would be a "People's Park". Berkeley police came and cleared out the park and later that day rioting broke out, lasting several weeks.

[7] It was rumored that the radical group, Weather Underground, was behind the killing, but this was never proven and the case was never solved.

[8] The author interviewed retired WCPD Sergeant Ron O'Dell for this story on 3/11/15. Officer Doug Silva's shattered police helmet remained in evidence at WCPD well into the 1990's and was seen there by the author.

[9] Source: 4/18/70 edition *of California Aggie*. U.C. Davis newspaper.

[10] Fonda can be seen talking about her trip to Vietnam in a Phil Donahue interview available on several sources on the internet. The returning POWs from Vietnam clearly told a different story about their treatment.

[11] Fonda didn't limit her activism to just the Vietnam War. She also supported the Black Panther Party and the American Indian occupation of Alcatraz, among other radical causes. Some have cited Fonda's youth as an excuse for her behavior. Fonda was 31 years old when she went to North Vietnam.

Chapter Twenty-Four

Viet Nam Veterans of Diablo Valley

Those who know Norm Mahalich certainly wouldn't categorize him as someone who is shy about expressing his beliefs. Nor is he one who sits back and waits for others to do things. Like many others, when he returned from Vietnam and left the Marine Corps, he was more concerned about the future than reliving the past. There were many things that he experienced during his two tours in Vietnam that were troubling, particularly the many friends he lost there. His transition to civilian life wasn't easy and at times, he found himself disgruntled and discouraged, but he coped and tried to move on, becoming an airline pilot.[1]

As time marched on, Norm joined the American Legion and Veterans of Foreign Wars (VFW) organizations. He found both to be good organizations, steeped in tradition. Both were also more formal than he liked. What he really wanted was an organization dedicated to Vietnam Veterans exclusively, something more local. He envisioned it to be informal. Norm wanted something fresh, something new, something local and something separate from other organizations. He decided to form such an organization. He formed the group for the Vets who had been there, but also in memory of his 54 friends and the 58,000 others who didn't come home. Forming a group was a way to keep their memories alive.

On February 28, 1991, the Viet Nam Veterans of Diablo Valley held their first meeting, a dinner meeting, with Philip Butler as the guest speaker. Phil was a POW in Vietnam and gave an inspirational presentation. There were about 20 in attendance. Prior to the meeting and listed on the flyer advertising the meeting, were some prospective goals for the new organization:

1. Socialize and network with other Valley professionals who served in Viet Nam
2. Improve the image of Viet Nam Veterans through our own actions and activities
3. Share the camaraderie and friendship from so many years ago[2]

That first meeting began with the Pledge of Allegiance, followed by a brief tribute and the lighting of a candle at an empty table, set for those who are still missing, the POW/MIA table. Soon others who had served in Vietnam heard of the group and it began to grow. This was an organization exclusively for Vietnam Vets.

Norm began giving presentations in local schools and to civic organizations about Vietnam, educating the public about the war and about the Vets who had served. He and others felt this education was an important element of what the group could do.

As time went on and word spread, the group continued to grow in size. The leadership baton was passed on to others. Marine aviator Bill Picton and Air Force Vet Ron Azarcon shared the group's enthusiasm and spearheaded the expansion of the organization, along with others, helping the membership grow in those early days. With each change in leadership, new ideas surfaced. The group that originally formed primarily to support each other, exchange experiences and to help create a better image for Vietnam Vets in the community, gradually evolved into a group that shifted its focus outward. Their focus was now on improving the community by helping Veterans who were in need.

As the Vets saw ways in which they could help other Veterans in the community, they found tremendous community support. As membership grew, so did the energy and enthusiasm to take on new tasks, to expand on ways to support other individual and community efforts. In turn, the community support for them grew by leaps and bounds.

One cornerstone to their success is that they have totally eliminated political, religious, military rank and commercial attachments from all aspects of their organization. This allows them to focus completely on Veteran needs and other projects and ways in which they choose to serve the community. Although they stand independently from other Veteran Service Organizations (VSO's), the groups support one another and have good working relationships.

Their first major project was just a concept when it began in 1991. Norm Mahalich felt there should be a local monument to honor Veterans from all wars, something that was lacking locally. For years he campaigned to get support for the project. The town of Danville donated land for it, but funding was needed for the material and construction of the monument. Fundraising projects were undertaken by the group over a period of several years. The "All Wars Memorial

Foundation" was established to move the project forward, incorporating local businessmen, Veterans and elected officials. The memorial was finally completed and dedicated on Memorial Day, May 30, 2005. It wouldn't exist today without Mahalich's concept and the continuing efforts of the group. VNVDV continues to host Memorial Day ceremonies at Oak Hill Park, where the memorial is located.[3]

Fig 103 - The first six presidents of VNVDV (L-R) Norm Mahalich, Bill Picton, Ron Azarcon, Rich Lambert, Mike McDaniel and Mike Weber (2004 photo)

Another major project started by the group is East Bay Stand Down. This is a biennial event that began in 1999, spearheaded by Vets Denver Mills and Jerry Yahiro. Mills became the first Executive Director and Yahiro was the first director. For these events more than 3,000 volunteers gather to provide a wide variety of services to as many as 500 needy and/or homeless Vets.

Fig 104- Vets and Volunteers at first Standdown (1999)

Veterans from the nine San Francisco Bay Area counties are invited to attend. They register and are pre-approved before the 4-day event starts. The attendees stay in tents with cots provided. They receive new clothing as needed and all meals are donated by business and civic groups. While there the Vets are offered or assisted in accessing a variety of services, including the following:

- Showers and haircuts
- Court services and legal aid
- Mental health services
- Dental care
- ID/Drivers licenses
- Transitional and permanent housing
- Medical care
- Emergency shelter
- VA HealthCare

All who participate are volunteers and funding is provided by donations. None of the funds are used for salaries, but go directly to assisting the Vets. The project has grown immensely since that first year, incorporating more services and gaining more support. Since 2012, Jerry Yahiro has been the sole director.

FIG 105 - DENVER MILLS, JERRY YAHIRO AND VOLUNTEER (STANDDOWN 2010)

The group is involved in multiple other projects. One of their two annual fundraisers is the Walk of Honor across the Alfred Zampa Memorial Bridge, which spans the Carquinez Strait in the San Francisco Bay Area. The bridge intersects Hwy 80, crossing from Crockett to Vallejo. This is a fundraising event where volunteers donate money in the name of a Veteran and walk as a group across the bridge, a distance of about 2/3 of a mile and back. It is held every year in May on Armed Forces Day. More than 500 volunteers participate in the event, which is followed by a luncheon. This event is sponsored by Phillips 66.

The other fundraiser is their annual crab feed, combined with a silent auction. Thousands of dollars are raised every year at this event to use in projects to help other Vets.

FIG 106 - VETS DAVE SMITH AND JEFF JEWELL TRAINING FOR ALCATRAZ SWIM (2016)

The group sponsors another fairly new and increasingly popular annual event, the "Take the Rock Veteran Swim Challenge", which began in 2013. This is a swim-training event, culminating in a swim from Alcatraz Island to Aquatic Park in San Francisco, a distance of 1.2 miles. The weekly training begins three months before the fall event. The swim is open to anyone who has served in the military and to their immediate family. Participants range in age from 12 to their early 70's, and include amputees and paraplegics. Nearly 50 swimmers participated in 2016.

Each year in June VNVDV sponsors a Veterans Retreat at a duck club in Yuba City, California. This weekend event is specifically for Gulf War Vets. 20 Gulf War Vets are selected for an all-expense paid weekend, where they can swim, shoot trap (no ducks, just clay pigeons), visit and relax in a stress-free environment. On Saturday, the Vietnam Helicopters

Museum brings their restored Huey helicopter to the club and takes the Vets for a ride and aerial tour of the region.[4]

Another event that has become a tradition is "Operation Santa Claus". The group selects a combination of 100 active military, Blue Star and Gold Star families and hosts a private Christmas party for these families, complete with Santa Claus and a nice gift for each child. Due to the size of the group there are actually two parties, in the morning and the afternoon. Needless to say, it is a popular and worthwhile event. Along with the toys, the event includes entertainment and food. It is sponsored by the Tesoro Golden Eagle Refinery, located in Avon, California.

Mike Martin and Bill Green have become the two co-directors of the Speakers Bureau. Through their efforts in the local schools, educating students on various aspects of the Vietnam War, they continue to provide a true and very personal account of the war, occasionally assisted by other members of the group. As of 2016, they have reached more than 72,000 San Francisco Bay Area students through their work. [56]

In 2006, the group, led by Vet Mike Weber's efforts, raised $15,000 in support of the Wheelchair Foundation, enough to buy 560 wheelchairs. Several Vets from VNVDV accompanied Wheelchair Foundation representatives to Vietnam that year, traveling throughout the country, supplying wheelchairs to the disabled, many of them children in orphanages who had severe physical and/or mental disabilities resulting from the effects of Agent Orange so many years before. In addition to the wheelchairs, they donated $3500 to schools and orphanages. Some of the Vets brought their spouses and all paid their own expenses. John

Reese, one of the Vets, also brought with him 60 pounds of medicines, which were donated to a children's clinic.

FIG 107 - MIKE WEBER ON RIGHT, DELIVERING WHEELCHAIR IN 2006

In 2012, additional funds were raised by the group for 320 more wheelchairs. A group of 17 Vets and spouses made the trip. While there they had the opportunity to meet a former enemy. Many of the Vets described these two trips as healing experiences.

Each year the group provides several thousand free flags to attendees of the July 4th parade in Danville, California. They support virtually every other worthwhile Veteran-oriented event in the San Francisco Bay Area.

One project they have supported for many years is "Operation Welcome Home". Since 9/11, the group has been active in supporting and attending celebrations for Vets returning home to the Bay Area. They do everything possible to insure that no Veteran will be left behind and that today's returning Vets will not have to face a similar return as they were given. They want every returning Vet to receive the dignity, honor and respect that he or she deserves.[7]

FIG 108 - VETS MEET WITH FORMER ENEMY IN VIETNAM (2012)

Today, the group still holds its monthly dinner meetings on the first Thursday of the month. There is still that same informal tone to the meetings, beginning with time for visiting, laughter and introductions. The formal meeting still begins with the Pledge of Allegiance, followed by a tribute to those still missing by the lighting of a candle at the POW/MIA table and a moment of silence. At the end of each meeting the candle is extinguished, accompanied by another moment of silence. So none of this has changed.

Despite some of these similarities to its origins, it has evolved into a much different organization since its inception. That small group of 20 who were at that very first meeting has grown to include 165 active members. Their original motto "Proudly we served" remains. Yet, although there have been some major changes, it maintains those same core values under which it began, held together by the same glue that formed it originally, which is the common bond of being Vietnam Vets and the pride they take in serving their community and their country. That part will never change.[8]

NOTES AND REFERENCES

[1] Read Mahalich's Vietnam story "Courage in Elephant Valley".

[2] These prospective goals are words taken from the flyer, but the actual wording is not in the by-laws.

[3] The All Wars Memorial is located at Oak Hill Park, 3005 Stone Valley Road, Danville, CA.

[4] No alcohol is allowed at this event.

[5] They began counting students in 2002. Although their primary focus is on schools, they have also provided presentations to various community organizations in the San Francisco Bay Area.

[6] Bill Green's story is "A Decent Proposal". Read more about Martin in "Welcome Home!."

[7] The group, by its involvement in Operation Welcome Home, hopes that younger Veterans will see the success of a grass roots organization like VNVDV and perhaps use it as a model in forming their own organization, so the tradition they have created will carry on to future generations.

[8] The Viet Nam Veterans of Diablo Valley are a non-profit corporation (501 c 19). The active members include 142 Vets who were in Vietnam and 23 wartime Vets who weren't actually in Vietnam.

Epilogue

The three men sat in the restaurant, visiting while they ate their meal. A casual observer may have thought they were related, but that was not the case. The two older men were related only by the commonality of experiences they had shared in a war zone nearly 50 years ago. The younger man was related by the friendship he now shared with one of these Vietnam Vets.[1]

For one of the Vets, Fred Granados, it was his first time meeting the younger man, Matt Payne, but he had information to share. The other Vet, Joe Callaway, was no stranger to Matt. They first met before, several years ago. That first meeting was a little awkward. Matt's father and Joe had been friends, close friends in Vietnam in 1967, when they were both young lieutenants and infantry platoon leaders in the 9th Infantry Division.

Matt's father, Herman "Chuck" Payne, was killed on April 26, 1967. Matt was born just two months earlier. His father never got to see him and Matt's only memories of his father are stories told to him by family…and from people like Joe and Fred. Joe's memories are particularly important because Joe was with Matt's father the night before he was killed.

The way in which Matt connected with Joe is a story by itself. Joe wrote a book about his personal experiences in Vietnam, *Mekong First Light: An Infantry Platoon Leader in Vietnam*. The book has sold well since it was first released in 2004. By chance, a friend of Matt's family read the book and told family members about references to Chuck Payne in it and of seeing Chuck's photo. Matt's older sister made the initial contact with Joe, leading to Matt's first contact with him.

FIG-109 -LT. JOE CALLAWAY ON LEFT   FIG 110-LT. CHUCK PAYNE 4/25/67

It wasn't as if Matt didn't know anything about his father. Matt's mother remarried, but Matt grew up with stories about his father shared by his mother, with the support and encouragement of his stepfather. Matt's aunt and others also shared stories of his father and Matt retained the family name, but there were other answers that Matt didn't have. How was his father perceived by his buddies in Vietnam? Was he a good leader? What were his last days like?

Matt did a lot of traveling for business and arranged to meet with Joe Callaway on a trip to California. During that first meeting Matt did get some answers from Joe. It was clear to Matt that Joe was a close friend of his father's and it was also clear that Joe still felt a tremendous sense of loss. Matt learned more about his father's last night.

Joe told Matt that he and his men flew in by helicopter that day. Chuck's platoon suffered several combat casualties and the wounded were flown out in the same helicopter that brought Joe in. The friends were happy to be together, if even for a short time in a war zone. After Joe landed, they began taking sniper fire. They found themselves taking cover behind a dike in a rice paddy. Chuck was laughing as they lay there, typical of his fearless approach to combat. Joe took the opportunity to snap a photo of his buddy as they lay there.

Matt learned that the two men stayed up late that night talking, having a few beers and reminiscing. Joe's platoon was relieving Chuck's platoon the next day and Chuck was going to a staff assignment. Despite the fact that Chuck was being taken out of combat, he spoke of lingering doubts about surviving the war. While it was true that their unit was experiencing heavy casualties, Chuck was being removed from his role as a platoon leader and going to a much safer assignment. He had just one more day left as a platoon leader.

Joe told Matt more about their conversations that night in the bunker. Chuck was ecstatic about the recent birth of his son, Matt, and they celebrated the birth. Chuck wanted badly to get home to his wife, his daughter and the son he'd never met. In two weeks he was going to meet his family in Hawaii for R&R, which was another cause for celebration. Joe was still sleeping when Chuck left the next morning. Chuck was killed later that same day.[2]

Matt knew how his father died, but through Joe he had a different connection to his father. They kept in touch after this first meeting. When Matt came to California on business trips, he made it a point to visit Joe.

On Matt's most recent trip, Joe brought Fred Granados to their meeting. Fred was assigned to Chuck's platoon as a combat medic soon after Chuck's death, replacing another medic killed in combat. Fred knew Chuck only through the stories of the soldiers who served under him, the grunts. When Fred joined the platoon he soon learned of the love and respect these men had for Lt. Payne, both as a man and as a leader, and of their great sense of loss when he was killed. Chuck's replacement clearly had some big shoes to fill. This is what he shared with Matt and Joe that night over dinner.

Matt doesn't meet with Joe for answers anymore. He has the available answers, but the connection to his father is still there and he can now pass this information on to his own two children. Now when they meet they talk about other things. A friendship has developed from that first meeting, an important one for both.

One might think that this connection Matt Payne and Joe Callaway have developed is unique. The individual circumstances and details are unique, but the concept of these Vets meeting and providing information to family members of their buddies lost in combat is far from unique. In fact, it's fairly commonplace, but it's not a topic that's discussed openly, at least not in most cases. As with many other things, it's just something they do.[3]

These meetings with families and loved ones aren't sponsored by the Viet Nam Veterans of Diablo Valley. The Vets just do it on their own. In nearly all cases it can be healing, but there is also pain involved, the pain of the memories. The Vets are involved individually in various other projects as well, such as mentoring combat Veterans from more recent conflicts and assisting Veterans in other ways, in some cases even financially to help them get on their feet again.

FIG 111 - MATT PAYNE AND JOE CALLAWAY

So the good deeds of the group aren't the only efforts of the members. They involve themselves in other worthwhile efforts, mostly without fanfare, and often (but not exclusively) to assist other Veterans.

These three words...duty...honor...country have often been used in reference to military service. If fact, these words are the motto of the U.S. Military Academy at West Point. The words received additional recognition and attention by General Douglas Macarthur in a 1962 speech he gave at West Point and they have been used almost exclusively in a military context since the earliest days of our country. Today they are used to represent the very best in our military, regardless of branch of service.

The Veterans in this book represent the commitment to our country represented in these words, not just in the stories of their military service but in what they are still doing today, collectively and individually. They didn't stop serving when their military service ended. They are not just observers. They are also leaders and active participants in making the world around them a better place for all of us.

You've read stories of just a few members of the Viet Nam Veterans of Diablo Valley, brief glimpses of a few minutes or at most a few hours, of their service in Vietnam. Yet all of the members served their country honorably during an extremely difficult period in our nation's history. They continue serving their communities and, in a larger sense, their country today. They consider it their duty and they continue to do it with honor. That's who they are. They are the Viet Nam Veterans of Diablo Valley.[4]

NOTES AND REFERENCES

[1] The two Vets, Joe Callaway and Fred Granados, served in the same company in Vietnam, during the same general time period, in different platoons. They did not meet until both became members of the Viet Nam Veterans of Diablo Valley.

[2] Chuck Payne, Joe Callaway and Fred Granados served in Company B, 2nd Battalion, 60th Infantry, 9th Infantry Division. See Fred Granados chapter "Halloween Ambush".

[3] This theme surfaced repeatedly during the author's interviews with Vets, more often than not when the author asked questions relating to contacting families of friends lost in combat.

[4] Joe Callaway was interviewed for this story on 11/23/16. Fred Granados was interviewed on 12/23/16 and Matt Payne was interviewed on 2/12/17.

Appendix A

The following sketches were all drawn by combat sketch artist Jim Hardy during his two Vietnam tours. The originals are property of the U.S. Army.

Fig 112-JOHN TURNER-238TH AVIATION COMPANY

Fig 113-SGT. BOBBY L. TRENT, 82ND AIRBORNE

Fig-114-DOC SARBECK, MEDIC 5TH MECHANIZED

Fig 115-SGT. THORNTON 5th MECHANIZED DIV

Fig 116-BUCKY SHIELDS, TROOP D 7/17TH CAVALRY DRIVER

**Fig 117-SGT. JAMES O'GARA, GUNSHIP
CREWCHIEF, "COWBOYS", 335TH AHC**

Figure 118-SP4 MIKE CARLSON, CO B, 299TH ENGINEERING BN

Fig 119-SP4 CLYDE PATTERSON, CO C, 199TH LIGHT INFANTRY

Fig 120-SGT. PERRY, CO A, 2/3 199TH LIGHT INFANTRY

Fig 121-SGT. ITO, CO A 2/3 199TH LIGHT INFANTRY

Fig 122-PFC. JOSEPH SANTOLOCITO CO C 2/3 199TH LIGHT INFANTRY

Fig 123-UNKNOWN SOLDIER WAITING TO GO HOME

APPENDIX B

The Body Count Continues
By Tucker Callaway

(Author's note: This is a story written in 1992 by Tucker Callaway, son of U.S. Army infantry platoon leader Joe Callaway, while a high school junior at San Ramon Valley High School in Danville, California. It provides a personal, thoughtful and unique insight on what it means to be the son of a Vietnam combat Vet.)[1]

I have always been curious about the Vietnam War and what happened there, what it was like to be there. My dad served in the war, and we periodically talk about Vietnam, but it is not a pleasant topic for him to discuss. I thought as

FIG 124-TUCKER CALLAWAY 1992

most people who have not experienced a war, that it would be filled with glory and heroism. This attitude brought many young men to the war. When I thought of the war, visions of valor and courage ran through my head. In my mind the greatest part of the whole war would be the joyous anticipation of the last week before the discharge and coming home. The night before, not being able to sleep and then finally the flight home...getting off the plane and running to your family who greet you with open arms. They are happy to see you alive and say how much they missed you. And the people who didn't serve would envy you and feel as if they missed something great.

What the Vietnam veterans went through was unique. It was a "once in a lifetime experience", something no one else could relate to without personally participating. The Vietnam War was many things to many people, but no one considered it great. A Vietnam vet named Billy Nascimento, who was a grunt tanker in the war, met with my dad at me at the Veteran's Center in Concord. This is a great place that my dad has visited periodically over the past several years. It is a sanctuary for vets. It is federally funded but given an autonomous status to separate it from the Veteran's Administration bureaucracy. Vietnam vets hate the V.A.[2]

We met in a room with three couches. It is normally used as a group meeting room. There was an "airplane mission" video game in the corner. The walls were clad with unit banners and camaraderie-type war pictures. The banners were of Army and Marine divisions and on a bulletin board were posted veteran-related newspaper articles. There was a large fish tank just outside the room. It was filled with many fish. Their colors showed ornately through the clear glass and clearer water. Not a speck of debris could be seen in the tank. I also noticed many smaller tanks around the office. They contained single fish such as Siamese fighting fish or gold fish. The counselors who work there, all of whom served in the Vietnam War, took pride in their care of fish.

The waiting room also contained a few green, well-watered plants. We were made to feel comfortable when we walked in. It was a very friendly and warm atmosphere. I asked Billy about his war experiences. He told me the many descriptions that follow. But most important was the point he stressed when he said, "The war was a horrible experience, but I am proud of what I did, and I would never give it up." "They were like young seedlings", Billy explained to me, "They were ripped out of their American soil and planted somewhere in Vietnam, a place foreign to each and every one of them". They knew little of the land or the war. Some of the boys were only 17 years old, while the average age was only 19 years.

Most had only been driving a little over two years and now they were driving tanks, carrying rifles and making decisions that could lead their whole platoon to death. Suddenly everything their mothers had tried to tell them for the last 19 years about being kind and not hurting other people was reversed. With their heads spinning they were given weapons and instructed to kill. Young men only 22 years old were commanding platoons of 42 men.

Billy tells a story of his first experience with death, when he and the men he was patrolling with, opened fire on movement in a bush. He was the first of the men to see the results. He saw, lying there, his first victims, a village girl of 15 years and her 8 year-old brother. Billy goes on to say he had to deny those feelings and there was no one to talk to about it. He had to be stoic. Everyone learned to deny their emotions and the guilt, but they remain, even today. This was only the first of many deaths this 19 year-old would experience, because this happened on his second day in combat.

As he told me his story, he described the dead bodies of the children and the bullet holes in their flesh, wounds of a nature he had only seen in horror films. His eyes seemed to be focused on the wall, but they were really focused somewhere in Vietnam over 25 years ago.

Kids just a year older than myself vowed to come out of the war somebody special, to come out a hero, but most came out in body bags. If a senior at our school died and everyone was watching, it would be a great shock. This occurred daily to young soldiers in Vietnam, many the same age as the seniors at San Ramon Valley High. Many had gone through a year of rigorous boot camp and training together and were all close friends and then suddenly, they started dying, sometimes one at a time, sometimes in groups.

Joseph Callaway Jr, a lieutenant, an infantry platoon leader and a Green Beret in Special Forces in Vietnam, describes the war as "going out with a group of friends in a car every day and looking for a head-on collision. You know at least one of you is going to die and it might be you." Billy nodded his head in agreement and told me to imagine myself two years from now with all my friends dying. Callaway told me a story of his friend choking on his own blood and dying of chest wounds while another friend lay only a few feet away with the top of his head blown off. The boys watched their friends mutilated all the way up to the day they left Vietnam.

Callaway said, "The Vietnam War was controlled by the politicians, fought by inexperienced kids and lacked military objectives. We tried to impose our country's will on a civil war. What was trying to be accomplished was very confusing. It was a street fight, a nasty and sometimes personal guerilla war. It created great conflict and guilt in our country. We all suffered, those who participated and those who did not. It divided families and friends, created hawks and doves, and more personal conflict for our country. The government created a draft system that forced the less advantaged to fight the war. This created more guilt and conflict. We all lost."

It was a Vietnam Tuesday night and Billy was to go home Wednesday afternoon. Within his platoon they drew straws to see which squad would patrol that night. Billy and his group were chosen to stay. Upon waking up in the morning Billy and the rest of the guys learned that last night the tank squad had driven right into an ambush and everyone was killed. Billy had to pick up the bodies. Two hours later he was on a plane going home.

On Friday, he was back in the States, sitting down, eating dinner with his family in Martinez, California. He sat there thinking about his friend's dead body in another world as his family asked what was wrong and said "welcome home". "Welcome home, f___ what?" Billy said, "My friend just died and it could have been me and now suddenly it is all over." He told me I probably shouldn't write that. I gathered it was uncustomary for him to swear in front of people he wasn't close to.

There was no welcome home for the veterans. Just as suddenly as the 18 year-old bodies and minds were shipped over there, 19 year-old bodies and 40 year-old minds were shipped back. There was nothing gradual about their return. They fought for their lives for a year and some much longer, and then they were home and safe after fighting a war practically the same day. Many were dumped off at northern California's Travis Air Force Base, and no one wanted to have anything to do with them. They were confused and greeted by no one but the anti-war protestors, who degraded their efforts.

Billy's descriptions reminded me of a song the rock group *Poison* sings about the vets, that they "fought a losing war on a foreign shore to find their country didn't want them back". There have been many songs written about this problem. Billy Joel, Bruce Springsteen, etc. sing them. They sing about sadness and agony and guilt. When a society is hurting you can often find it in its music.[3]

Billy continued, saying when they returned from Vietnam they couldn't cope. Most couldn't adjust or just didn't belong to a structured society. A high percent of our homeless population is Vietnam vets. There is one vet who goes to the Concord Veterans Center who has been homeless since 1970, the day he returned from Vietnam. He wouldn't have it any other way. He feels insecure if he's not in the bush. Most become isolationists. If they had friends, they were other vets, but most were without friends. They found they had nothing in common with their old friends. Their families were afraid of them.

Billy slept in a corner with no blankets with his .45 pistol, which he took everywhere with him, close at hand. They were unwanted and labeled "crybabies", "whiners", and people said "They couldn't fight a war right". Billy told me all this in a private counsel room where he works at the Concord Veterans Center. I looked at his large body and stern face, and looked again into his eyes. They were sky blue and soft. Looking past the sternness and size of this man into his eyes I saw the light glisten in the corner of his eye and noticed the beginning of a tear. He said, "People who have been through a war care more because they have more experiences, and know how fragile life is".[4]

Jack Keegan has been a friend of my family for over 20 years. When my parents lived in Massachusetts, before I was born, my dad worked for W.R. Grace, a multi-national chemical company. Jack worked for my dad. Jack now owns his own electrical motor manufacturing rep business. He told us over dinner that he had just bought controlling interest in the company. He visits from Los Angeles on business and spends the night about once or twice every few months. We often talk about colleges. He has two children in college. His son, Johnny, attends Northern Arizona and his daughter, Jenna, who should still be a high school senior, is in her first semester at Saddleback Junior College. Next year she will be in pre-med at the University of Colorado. Jack has researched many colleges and has insightful information for me.

We were just finishing dinner and I questioned him on what it was like to return home from Vietnam and if it was hard for him. He was reluctant to answer my questions. Jack said, "Returning home was an awful experience for most vets, but not for all." He was an A-6 Intruder Navy pilot in Vietnam and returning was not as bad for him. His war was high tech, very impersonal. As a strategic night bomber he flew his missions at low levels at incredible speeds. He flew through anti-aircraft flak, Soviet SAMS (surface to air missiles) and ground fire. He only saw fellow pilots' planes go down, and he never personally saw the damage his bombs inflicted. It was all detached.

He told me his squadron went over as a unit and they returned together on their aircraft carrier. It took them over a month to get back to the States. He returned to a naval community. He said the hardest part was seeing the families of those who had died, because the community was so close knit. But he had a strong support group because he was living in a community with his war friends. Jack seemed much more emotionally detached than Billy or my dad. His answers were short and to the point. It seemed as if going any deeper was something he was not willing to think about.

It was not as easy for the infantry soldiers. "They came back to the States questioning themselves and feeling insecure," said Billy. "They had many problems that the government was unwilling to deal with." Many suffered and are still suffering from mental problems, such as Post Traumatic Stress Disorder. This was the biggest problem the government ignored. The veterans who suffered this were labeled "psychotic", Billy said. Many became alcoholics and drug addicts. Their suicide rate was very high. They look for escapes because they cannot adjust and fit back into our society. Many veterans have not come to grips with their problems, but those who have can deal with themselves, according to Billy.

Billy says he has gone to bed every night for more than 20 years with the vision of his dead friend's face in his mind. I could tell that the vision of his friend was in his head how. He shook his head as if coming out of a trance and continued, "Veterans have an enemy within them. There is a primal rage that the war has created in them. It is from the extreme fear, brutality, guilt, sadness, rejection and frustration in the war experience and it affects our whole society. Humanity carries this rage from many centuries of war." In most Vietnam veterans it has become subdued, but Joe Callaway describes the anger and memories as "baggage". They are carried with you no matter where you go. These men carry an emotional rage within them. It can be taken out on other people, but it is directed 20 years in the past.

My uncle Rick was a lieutenant in Vietnam and in the 1968 Tet offensive had one leg shot off below the knee, the other paralyzed below the knee and a little finger shot off. He was on the battlefield four hours before medical evacuation. He had to tourniquet his wounds to prevent bleeding to death. Life has been difficult and frustrating for him. My dad said, "He has tremendous courage and determination. He is determined never to give up."

Two summers ago we were at a mountain lake beach. There were many people at the beach. My brothers, nephews, friends and I were swimming. Uncle Rick had his bathing suit on under his pants. He laid down his cane, took off his pants, his left prosthetic leg and his right knee brace and crawled to the water. He is a great swimmer. He did this to let me and my brothers know about his leg wounds, to have fun in the water like everyone else and to prove to everyone around that his physical problems did not matter.

Eventually, he had to crawl back up the beach to put on his equipment to walk again. I was amazed, shocked and proud when I saw this. I had never seen a disabled person struggle without their support apparatus before. I thought I would be embarrassed to have a disabled relative struggling like that on a public beach, covered with sun-tanned girls I wanted to meet. My reaction was just the opposite. I couldn't have been more proud, for my uncle, my family and every person who served in the war.

Seeing him crawl into the lake and crawl out touched my soul. I will always remember him by that. I will respect him more just for going swimming than anything else he will ever do. My uncle Rick will carry his psychological and physical wounds of war to his death. His therapy is teaching English in junior high school in New Canaan, Connecticut, the town he and my dad grew up. He is very intelligent, very resourceful and a Harvard graduate.

The vets will always carry with them the sadness, guilt and the gruesome memories, but they will also carry the pride in what they did and that they did their best. My dad, Joe Callaway, explained to me, "Never in my life will I have as much responsibility as I did then, I will never be as proud of myself or love myself more for what I did, except for my family, and there is also nothing I have done which I hate myself more for participating in."

The casualties of war are all around me. My trip to the Concord Veterans Center was enlightening. It helped me understand better the people around me. These strong-willed men are haunted by the war. Many Vietnam vets dropped out and refuse responsibility. Many are still fighting the war within themselves. One important fact I learned at the Concord center was the final casualties of the Vietnam War are these vets' families-the marriages and children.

I, too, am counted in the casualties. My life is vastly different from my friends who didn't have a father in the war. Everything I do is translated to a bigger picture. It comes to a point where a 3.8 grade point average with three honors courses isn't always good enough. A 3.8 in the mind of a combat platoon leader means you made one mistake and one mistake causes death. The years before college have been an intense boot camp to prepare me for the war of life. My dad will make sure I can overcome any obstacle. It is probably all to my benefit, but it sure hasn't been a comfortable ride.

My dad is excellent at training men. He now trains and manages engineer/MBAs in business. There is a time between becoming a teenager and leaving for college when I just want to be a carefree kid. I want to stay out real late or go away for a weekend with my friends without any worries. My dad is very protective and likes to control everything I do. He knows how easily and quickly life can slip away. But just as my dad and the many other veterans wouldn't trade in their experiences in the war, I would never change the experiences I've had with him. There is no man in my life I have hated more, but there is also no man I will ever love more for all he has done for me. As I understand my dad better, I understand myself better.

The cost of this terrible tragedy and other wars will always continue to increase. Long after the war has ended, the body count continues.[5]

FIG 125-LT. JOE CALLAWAY WITH VIETNAMESE CHILDREN, JAN 1967 BINH SON, VIETNAM

NOTES AND REFERENCES

[1] Joseph W. Callaway Jr. was an infantry platoon leader in the 1st Platoon, Company C, 2nd Battalion, 60th Infantry, 9th Infantry Division.

[2] The feelings about the V.A. have changed among some of the Vets since this story was written in 1992, but some Vietnam Vets still harbor these feelings and don't avail themselves of V.A. benefits. The Concord Vet Center is still in existence today, providing a variety of services at no cost for Veterans. (See Foreword by Jeff Jewell, Director of Concord Vet Center.)

[3] The song lyrics are from the glam metal band Poison song *Something to Believe In*, written and sung by Poison on their 1990 album Flesh & Blood on the Enigma label of Capitol Records.

[4] William Paul Nascimento, a Marine Corps Veteran, passed away on April 6, 2003 at the age of 55 years. (Source-Contra Costa Times obituary, dated April 17, 2003)

[5] Tucker Callaway later attended U.C. Berkeley where he graduated with a degree in computer science.

Photo and Illustration Contributors

Bibliography and References

Books

Barnes, Thornton D. *Migs Over Nevada: Mig Exploitation Projects at Area 51.* CreateSpace Publishing, 2015

Baskir, Lawrence and Strauss, William. *Chance and Circumstance: The Draft, the War and the Vietnam Generation.* New York, NY, Vintage Books, 1978.

Burns, Richard R. *First In, Last Out.* New York, NY, Presidio Press, 2002.

Carpenter, Stephen. *Boots on the Ground: The History of Project Delta.* CreateSpace Publishing, 2010.

Calloway, Joseph W. Jr. *Mekong First Light: An Infantry Platoon Leader in Vietnam.* New York, NY, Presidio Press, 2004.

Donovan, David, *Once A Warrior King: Memories Of An Officer in Vietnam.* New York, NY, McGraw-Hill, 1985.

Haslam, Tim. *Stars & Stripes And Shadows: How I Remember Vietnam.* Bloomington, Indiana. AuthorHouse, 2007.

Ketwig, John. *And A Hard Rain Fell: A GI's True Story of the War in Vietnam.* New York, NY, Macmillan, 1985.

Knott, Richard. *Fire from the Sky: Seawolf Gunships in the Mekong Delta.* Annapolis, MD. Naval Institute Press, 2005.

Morris, Ray. The Ether Zone: U.S. Army Special Forces Detachment B-52, Project Delta. Ashland, OR, Hellgate Press, 2009

Santoli, Al, *To Bear Any Burden.* New York, NY, E.P. Dutton, 1985.

Vetter, Lawrence C. Jr, *Never Without Heroes: Marine 3rd Reconnaissance Battalion in Vietnam (1965-70)* New York, NY, Ballantine, 1996

U.S. Government Archival Information

1st Squadron, 4th Cavalry, After Action Reports 1968, Department of the Army, Headquarters 1st Squadron, 4th Cavalry, APO San Francisco 96345

3rd Marine Recon Battalion, Fleet Marine Force Pacific, Command Chronology Report, February 1966, National Archives

3rd Marine Recon Battalion, Company A, 3rd Platoon Patrol Report, February 22, 1966, National Archives

3rd Military Police Battalion, Fleet Marine Force Pacific, Command Chronology Report, 1969, National Archives

2nd Battalion, 9th Marine Regiment, Command Chronology Report, September 1967, National Archives

71st Evacuation Hospital (SMBL) Hospital Mass Casualty Evacuation Report-Battle of Dak To (November 1967)

BARREL ROLL, 1968-73: An Air Campaign in Support of National Policy, by Colonel Perry L. Lamy, USAF, Air War College, Air University, Maxwell Air Force Base, Alabama, 10 May 1995

Command History of Helatktron 3 for Calendar Year 1970 (April 13, 1971), submitted by Captain Martin Twite

Granados, Frederick, Specialist 4, U.S. Army, Company B, 2nd Battalion, 60th Infantry, Citation for Army Commendation Medal with "V" Device, for combat action on October 31, 1967

History of the 281st Aviation Company (Assault Helicopter) 10th Aviation Battalion (Combat) 1st Aviation Brigade 1 January 1969-31 December 1969, Prepared by Warrant Officer Douglas W. Jones

Lambert, Richard Warren, Lt. J.G. HA(L)-3, (Helicopter Attack Squadron (Light) 3, U.S.N.R., Bronze Star Citation for combat action on September 15, 1970

Ledford, Kenneth Jr, 1st Lt, 58th Medical Battalion, 68th Medical Group, U.S. Army, Navy Cross Citation for combat action on September 15, 1970

Official History of the 155th Aviation Assault Company, Operation Sam Houston After Action Report, March 16, 1967

Operation Sam Houston After Action Report, conducted by the 4th Infantry Division 1 January 1967-5 April 1977

U.S. Army General Order 3212, Distinguished Service Cross Citation for Richard Sperling

Historical Reviewed Articles

Air and Space Magazine, *Escape to U Taphao* (by Ralph Wetterhahn), January 1997

Air Mobility Command Museum, *Operation Babylift* (by Daniel L. Haulman)

Ban me Thuot Barb (155th Assault Company Newsletter), February 1999

Dragon News (52nd Aviation Company publication), March 26, 1967

Journal American Aviation Historical Society, *Battle at VC Lake*, Winter, 1988

Unpublished Private Documents

Corbett, Thomas (USMC). Personal summary of military and Vietnam experiences, 1967-1972

Green, Bill (USA). Journal of Vietnam experiences, 1967-1968

Ferguson, John Kirk (CDR USN) Strike Assault Boat Squadron 20 (Stabron 20) Unknown date

Kiper, Bill (USN). Flight log from February 1968

Laterra, Joseph (USMC), Statement of facts, dated April 3, 2004, regarding February 22, 1966 combat mission

Mahalich, Norman (USMC). Statement of facts dated October 1, 2001 regarding February 22, 1966 combat mission

Mahalich, Norman (USMC). Letter to Joseph Laterra, dated September 10, 1997, regarding February 22, 1966 combat mission

Mahalich, Norman (USMC). Flight log of combat missions in Vietnam.

Rider, Joseph (USMC). Statement of facts, dated August 22, 2003, regarding February 22, 1966 combat mission

Smith, David (USN). Personal letters to his fiancé, Jan, dated April 29, 1975, April 30, 1975, May 1, 1975, May 3, 1975 and May 15, 1975, describing events at U-Tapao Thailand and Andersen Air Force Base, Guam.

Index

A

A-1 Skyraider 55,233,
Agent Orange
iii,9,203,205,224,
Alcatraz 240,244,247,259
Anderson AF Base 235
An Loc 210
APC 116
Armstrong, Neil ix
Army Artist Team #9 209
A Shau 146,149
Azarcon, Ron 254,256

B

B-52 bombers 220,232,235
Baez, Joan 242
Bangkok, Thailand ix
Ban Me Thuot 47,58,296
Baratko, Robert 180,182
183,185
Baucom, Mike 49,53-55
Bauman, George 17,19
Beard, Charles C. 122
Behring, David i-iv,3
Beltran, Albert 215
Ben Het 11-14

Bien Hoa 83
Black Liberation Army 245
Black Panther Party 240-
256,251
Bozeman 137,138

C

C-47 35,157,233
C-123 69
C-130 15,233
Callaway, Joe 265-
270,280,287
Callaway, Tucker 277-287
Camp Pendleton 193-195
198,208
Camp Enari 39,40,44
Carlson, Mike 274
Cavite City 157,158
CH-46 32
China Beach 191
Christie, Dennis
Christobal, Bill 49,52
53,55,58
Cleaver, Eldredge 242,243
Concord Vet Center v,vi

The Author

This is Jerry Whiting's sixth book. Born in Sioux Falls, South Dakota he moved to Pleasant Hill, California (San Francisco Bay Area) when he was in high school. He obtained a Bachelor's Degree at U.C. Santa Barbara and later a Master's degree at John F. Kennedy University. He worked as a  counselor for a few years and then began a 25+ year career in law enforcement, working in a variety of assignments including patrol and the detective bureau. He was also a hostage/crisis negotiator during the last 15 years of his career. During this time he had the unique opportunity to work with several European police departments. In addition, he worked on a special project with the tribal police on the Cheyenne River Sioux Indian Reservation in South Dakota.

Jerry has always enjoyed investigating history, culminating in his first book, *I'm Off To War, Mother, But I'll Be Back*. He ultimately took an early retirement to pursue his passion, resulting in other books, including *Don't Let the Blue Star Turn Gold, Veterans in the Mist*, and *Of Broad Stripes and Bright Stars*. In addition, he published *Missions by the Numbers*, a group history of the 485th Bomb Group, a group that flew B-24 bombers out of Italy. Along the way he found the time to produce two documentaries, *In the Shadow of Mt. Vulture* and *New Year's At Ramitelli: A Safe Haven for Change*. The Ramitelli documentary tells the story of a unique relationship between one American bomb group and the Tuskegee Airmen. All of his previous works are about WWII and are non-fiction.

His interest began while researching his father's story, resulting in that first book. He became the Historian for his father's bomb group association. During the research for some of his books, while working with European researchers, he located aircraft crash sites that were previously undiscovered, some with remains of American servicemen. This information was shared with the Dept. of Defense, resulting in the recovery of remains.

Several years ago Jerry was invited to the Pentagon to give a training seminar to Dept. of Defense investigators on locating MIA's. This is a topic close to his heart and in March 2016 he cohosted a conference in Krakow, Poland which resulted in the gathering of some of the best European researchers with Dept. of Defense MIA investigators.

Jerry is often called upon as a guest speaker and has spoken to groups in Germany, Italy and Poland, as well as in venues across the United States. He and his wife live in Walnut Creek, California. This is his first book on Vietnam. All of his books are available on Amazon.com and are available on Kindle. Jerry can be reached through his email at **EAJWWhiting@aol.com**.

Suggested Readings

All of the following books have been written by Vets from the Viet Nam Veterans of Diablo Valley and are good reading.

Compass and A Camera: A Year in Vietnam, Steve Burchik This is Steve's personal memoir of a year spent in Vietnam, June 1968 to June 1969, as an infantry forward observer in the 1st Infantry Division. (2014)

Focus on Vietnam, Steve Burchik. Steve's first book is a memoir of his experiences in Vietnam. Steve was an avid photographer and this, his second book, is a book of photos he took while in Vietnam, a glimpse into the day to day life of an infantryman. (2016)

Mekong First Light: An Infantry Platoon Leader in Vietnam, Joseph W. Callaway Jr. This is Joe's personal memoir of his time in Vietnam, beginning with his assignment as an infantry platoon leader with the 9th Infantry Division in December 1966 and ending with his time as a staff officer with the 5th Special Forces in July 1968. (2004)

Stars & Stripes and Shadows: How I Remember Vietnam, Tim Haslam. This is Tim's account of his year spent as an infantryman in Vietnam, March 1968-March 1969, with the 4th Infantry Division. (2007)

Through My Eyes: A Story of Hope, Bob Whitworth. This is Bob's story of his time in Vietnam as an infantryman, beginning in 1968, where he served with the Americal Division (23rd Infantry). (2012)

Made in the USA
San Bernardino, CA
24 June 2019